1158

EMPOWERMENT THROUGH ENTERPRISE

Empowerment through Enterprise

A training manual
for non-government organizations

MALCOLM HARPER

INTERMEDIATE TECHNOLOGY PUBLICATIONS 1996

Intermediate Technology Publications
103/105 Southampton Row, London WC1B 4HH, UK

A CIP catalogue record for this book
is available from the British Library

ISBN 1 85339 332 0

Typesetting by J&L Composition Ltd, Filey, North Yorkshire, UK
Printed in UK by SRP, Exeter

Table of Contents

	Page
Acknowledgements	vii
What is this book for, and how should it be used?	1
Day One	
1. Introduction, our strengths, weaknesses and responsibilities	7
2. Our own views, and where do we stand now? The enterprise experience	14
3. How to generate business ideas	20
4. Planning for business	24
Day Two	
1. Business plan presentations	28
2. The financial reality of an enterprise	32
3. The 'dynamic balance sheet'	40
4. The practical use of business figures	49
Day Three	
1. How to obtain business information in the field	59
2. and 3. Group meetings with business owners	65
4. Presentation skills	66
Day Four	
1. and 2. Business presentations	68
3. What are NGOs, and what is their role in enterprise development?	71
4. Women in micro-enterprise	75
Day Five	
1. Group or individual enterprises?	80
2. Group enterprises — when and how?	85

	Page
3. Introduction to marketing	90
4. Marketing applications	94
Day Six	
1. Quality and efficiency	100
2. Record keeping	103
3. What do goods and services cost? Part 1	107
4. What do goods and services cost? Part 2	111
Day Seven	
1. Rates of return and the cost of money	115
2. The cost of NGO services	120
3. Marketing for NGOs	125
4. Self-help groups and the marketing of credit	130
Day Eight	
1. The Grameen Bank, Bangladesh	137
2. Micro-credit — who does what?	144
3. Self-sustainability for NGOs	149
4. Financial appraisal of NGOs	152
Day Nine	
1. Finance and strategy for NGOs	159
2. The enterprise experience: conclusion	163
3. Evaluation	165
4. Preparing and presenting proposals	169
Day Ten	
1. Preparing proposals, continued	171
2. and 3. What next?	175
4. Course evaluation and follow-up	177
Day Eleven	
1. Summary and conclusion	180

ACKNOWLEDGEMENTS

This book is based on over twenty years of experience of training and working with men and women from all over the world to assist poor people to improve their condition through self-employment and enterprise. The thousands of people who have sometimes benefited, and often suffered, from my efforts are the main source of the ideas in the book, and it would obviously be impossible to mention them all by name.

I should like, however, to express my gratitude to my colleagues at Cranfield, who may recognise some of their own training methods in these pages, and to colleagues from many other institutions with whom I have worked. I should in particular thank the Ford Foundation, whose offices in Africa and India have played a very important role in encouraging and supporting our work with non-government organizations, and the staff of the Kenya Institute of Management, the Foundation for Enterprise and Entrepreneurship Development in South Africa, the Arab Foundation for Enterprise Development in Egypt and the Xavier Institute of Management in India. Their ideas, and their criticism and suggestions, have been essential to the evolution of my own approach to teaching enterprise development.

Certain individuals have played a particularly important role. Jackie Bilton at Cranfield helped me to evolve the whole concept of training material, which has been applied in so many fields during the seventeen years we have worked together. My wife Uschi Kraus-Harper has perhaps been more critical, and thus more constructive, than most of my colleagues. Jon Westborg, first as a research student and later as a collaborator in his position as head of NORAD in New Delhi, suggested the whole process of writing, testing, revision and publication which has, I hope, ensured that at least the most obvious errors have been omitted, while his colleague Tara Sharma effectively managed the process, and me, which I know to be no easy task.

Above all, however, I must acknowledge the contribution made by the following participants in the first trial of the material in India in May 1994, and who then further tested it in their own institutions. Their work was then skilfully co-ordinated by Chandramauli Pathak of ICECD.

They are: Dharamvir Singh, RUCHI; V. Satyabati, PREM; Iqbal S. Kaundal, SUTRA; Raman Jaggi, EDI(I); Dinesh Acharya, Urmul Trust; Usha Raghunath, SAMPARK; Indra Bhatia, RAJCON; Emmanuel Pathil, RTDDA; Senoo Rawat, Haryana Social Work and Research Centre; Sanjukta Satapathy, PIPAR; S. Suryanarayana, Seva in Action; Rabindra Nath Sabat, FARR; G. Vasantha, Institute for Youth and Development; and Raghavendra S. Okade, AWAKE.

Finally, I should like to acknowledge the silent and gentle inspiration of Ilse Kraus, at whose bedside much of the first draft was written.

What is this book for, and how should it be used?

What is the book about?

This is a trainers' manual, which has been written to help you, the trainer, to provide useful training for NGO staff and others whose job it is to assist poor people to start or sustain micro-enterprises.

It is not primarily a manual for training micro-enterprise owners themselves, who are in any case often illiterate and rarely have time for full-time training, nor is it an ordinary book about how to assist micro-enterprises. As you will see, it is a training guide, with detailed step-by-step descriptions of some 40 sessions, which together make up a ten and a half day course on developing micro-enterprise.

The session guides are the main part of this book, and they are intended to be self-explanatory. This brief introductory section merely gives some information about its origins and purpose, who should use it, to train whom, and how to use it.

Why has the book been written?

In recent years, voluntary or non-government organizations (called NGOs throughout) have started to play an important role in helping poor people to increase their incomes through micro-enterprises. NGOs have always been involved in providing welfare services for the poor, but if poor people are to become independent they must earn more income. It is very difficult for people without education to find employment, anywhere, and self-employment, or micro-enterprise, is thus the only option for millions of poor people.

The Enterprise Development Centre at Cranfield School of Management in England started training courses in enterprise development, that is, how to assist people who are self-employed or wish to start small businesses, in 1977. At first, nearly all the participants came from government organizations, and most of them were involved in assisting formal small enterprises, which might aim to employ five or ten people, to borrow money from a bank and to use some modern machinery.

As the years went by, however, more of the participants came from NGOs, and they were interested in the smallest economic activities of poor people, who would probably never employ anybody apart from one or two family members, and for whom formal bank loans were an impossible dream. In 1987, therefore, with assistance from the Ford Foundation, we started a new course called 'Developing Income-generating Enterprise', which was designed specially for NGO staff who were working with micro-enterprises.

This course was very popular, and it satisfied a real need. It was, however, expensive, mainly because participants had to travel to England to attend it. The local environment was also not exactly relevant to the topic of micro-enterprises for the poor. Cranfield has always emphasized the application of learning, and we try to include field studies in every course, but there are not very many informal micro-enterprises, or agencies trying to assist them, in rural England.

Several of the participants in this course were already offering similar training in their own countries, and in order to overcome the problems of expense and the irrelevance of the environment, we started to work with institutions in a number of different countries so that locally appropriate versions of the course would be available less expensively to larger numbers of people than would ever be able to come to Cranfield.

Over time, we evolved a number of different training approaches to helping participants learn the various skills that are

1

needed for effective enterprise development for the poor, and it seemed appropriate to try to convert our own informal teaching notes into a more comprehensive form so that other trainers would be able to share them and make use of whatever ideas seemed to be useful. This book is the result of our effort to share our own enterprise development training ideas with other trainers.

What subjects are covered in the book?

The table of contents and the session guides themselves should be self-explanatory, but it may also be useful to give an overview as to why certain topics have been included, and, perhaps more importantly, why others have not.

NGOs are themselves enterprises; they are usually established in order to address certain local or national issues of concern to their founders, and not just to provide an income for their staff, but they still have to manage their affairs, to market their services, and in particular to account for their money, like any business. In fact, because the money they use is usually not their own but has been entrusted to them by individuals or institutions, they have a greater obligation than a private business to use their money wisely, and to be able to show others how they are using it.

Many NGOs are themselves badly mismanaged. They do not have up-to-date accounts; they do not have accurate records of who owes them money; they fail to communicate effectively with their clients and with their donors. This is serious for any NGO, whatever field it works in, but it is even more important that staff who are engaged in training and advising poor people to start and run micro-enterprises should themselves be able to demonstrate the same skills in the management of their own organizations.

For this reason, the sessions in the ten and a half day course which is described in this book lead from consideration of the management of micro-enterprises to the management of NGOs themselves. If somebody is good at advising poor people about simple business management, she should also be able to manage her own organization effectively, and vice versa. We must be able to practise what we preach.

Some readers may notice that there are no sessions about rapid or participatory rural appraisal, or about needs assessment, or indeed about project appraisal itself. This is partly because there are already many excellent training manuals covering these subjects, and partly because we believe that some techniques are over-used, because so many NGOs feel that they need to find out what people need in order to re-define their needs and then to tell them what to do.

This book is based on what we feel to be a more genuinely 'participatory' approach, in that it aims to help train NGO staff to enable poor people to do what they themselves want to do. We believe that most poor people know more than outsiders do about what sorts of enterprises they should start, and how they should be managed. What they need is access to resources to enable them to do what they know they can do, and this book is basically about training NGO staff and others to provide that access.

Who should use the book?

This book is for anyone who wishes to train others to assist poor people to increase their incomes through micro-enterprise. The emphasis is on training for NGO staff, but many other institutions are now becoming involved in assisting micro-enterprises, and some parts of the book will be useful for training government staff, bankers or employees of larger private enterprises which run programmes to help micro-enterprises. Their trainers, who will use this book, may be employed as staff trainers in the training department of one NGO, or as trainers in an institution which offers training for staff of many different NGOs or other institutions involved in this field.

Many trainers are not familiar with train-

2

ing guides of this sort, and some may even feel threatened or insulted by the implication that they can improve their courses by using ideas that others have provided. It is important to stress that the book does not aim to supplant or replace the trainers' own ideas or experience, but to complement them.

We have attempted in the session guides to give guidance both on the subject matter and the training methods, so that people with little previous training experience, or with little knowledge of micro-enterprise development, will be able to make good use of it. We also expect, however, that very experienced trainers, who have themselves worked for many years in micro-enterprise development, will also find many of the ideas useful.

Many NGOs do not have specialized training departments or trainers. The session guides can also be used by informal groups of field-workers who wish to improve their skills without the guidance of a trainer. The emphasis is very much on shared learning, and the role of the instructor can equally well be taken by a temporary chairperson who is herself a member of the group who wishes to be trained.

The session guides are not specifically designed for self-instruction, and many of the learning exercises depend on interaction between a number of people. Nevertheless, it is also possible to read and learn from this book on your own, rather like a programmed text.

Any trainer who wishes to use the session guides for training other people must of course read them through carefully beforehand, and work through the various exercises and case-studies on his own. This process will not only prepare him to train others with the material, but will also help him to learn new skills, attitudes and techniques. The advance preparation process alone can be very productive.

Many NGO trainers, as well as the people they train, are unfamiliar with finance and accounting, and they may even be nervous about dealing with calculations of any sort.

This manual is written for such trainers, and their trainees, and trainers who are qualified accountants may have more difficulty because they find it difficult to deal with finance in the simple ways which this manual suggests. It may be tempting to ask an accountant to deal with sessions such as the one on the financial reality of an enterprise (Day One — Session Two). It is far better, however, to try to understand the material yourself and, if necessary, to ask for guidance before conducting the session from someone with more experience. This whole course is based on the concept of shared learning. People will learn more from a trainer who admits that she herself is learning with them than from someone who 'knows it all', and who may not be able to communicate with those who are not so fortunate.

Who should be trained?

The training guides in this book should be useful for training anyone whose work involves assisting poor people's efforts to improve their incomes through self-employment. The emphasis is on NGO staff, but much of this material has been found to be useful for bankers, for staff of government departments, for volunteers, for the staff of international development agencies and for trainers and teachers themselves.

Several of the exercises were first developed in courses for business owners themselves, and although they are presented here in the context of a course for people who are assisting business owners, they can easily be extracted and used in business training courses.

The course in Developing Income-generating Enterprise from which this material has evolved was originally designed for middle-level NGO staff whose work involved regular contact with their clients. The material has also been used, however, for training people of many other levels of age and seniority, ranging from adult postgraduate students and senior bankers and civil servants to secondary or even primary schoolchildren.

Effective NGOs work through the participation of their clients, and they should themselves be participative organizations, where staff at every level are encouraged to contribute to important decisions. One of the main reasons why government organizations and banks have so often failed to empower the poor is that they themselves do not empower their own staff. NGOs are different, and this course is designed to enable senior and junior staff to work and learn together.

Some people may feel that some of the material is not relevant to them, either because they think (usually wrongly) that 'they know it all', or that the particular tasks are not their responsibility. If at all possible, the course should be used to break down hierarchical barriers of this sort, and participants should be drawn from all levels of their organizations.

The sequence of the course moves from clients' micro-enterprises through to the appreciation of NGOs themselves as enterprises, and the sessions from Day Seven — Session Two to Day Ten could be used with some modification as a short course, or part of a course, in NGO management. If some senior management cannot attend the whole ten and a half day programme, and if they really are genuinely familiar with the topics covered in the first six days (which many are not), they may be asked to join the course for the last four days only.

How should the book be used?

Anyone who wants to use this material must first read it through carefully, and decide what parts he wishes to use, and what changes or adaptations are needed. It is unlikely that many trainers will wish to use the whole manual as it stands. Some parts will be omitted, others will be substantially changed to take account of local circumstances, and other material may need to be added. Although the sessions are presented as a continuous 10-day course, individual sessions, or parts of sessions, can also, of course, be used on their own.

The session guides are written in some detail, but the instructor should not follow it slavishly. The overall theme of each session might be likened to a basic tune. Each player must interpret it as she thinks fit, leaving out some parts, adding others, and varying the sequence, the methods and the pace according to her individual preferences and skills, the needs of the group and the moment-by-moment situation in the classroom.

The course may not be able to be conducted in English, and NGO staff should realize that it is far more important for them to be able to communicate with their clients in their own local languages than to be able to follow a training course in English. In that case, of course, all the hand-outs will have to be translated before the course starts.

Even if the course can be given in English it will probably be necessary to make changes to the names, crops, sums of money and other aspects of many of the case-studies and exercises, and you should also remember that the best examples are those which come from the participants' or your own experience. Whenever possible, you should replace the examples given here by more locally relevant material of that kind.

Most of the hand-outs are case-studies or other working papers. There are very few summaries of what has been learned, and some trainers, and participants, may feel the necessity for reminders of this sort. They have been omitted deliberately, because we have found that participants sometimes think it does not matter if they fail to understand something during the session, since they can read up on it later. They very rarely do this, of course, and we feel it is better for participants to make and keep their own notes as reminders.

You should not fall into the trap of believing that you need less preparation time because you are working with pre-prepared training guides. You have to read through the material very slowly and carefully, several times, to be sure that you understand it yourself, to identify the places where changes are needed, and to think through every possible way in which participants may answer the many questions and exercises that are included, so that you will be able to respond appropriately.

It is much quicker and easier to prepare for a traditional one-way lecture session, because all you have to do is to decide what you are going to say. In participative training of the sort covered in these session training guides, you have to prepare for a whole range of different eventualities, many or even none of which may actually occur.

The management of each session must also be carefully planned. Some handouts or displays may have to be prepared and when necessary translated in advance; participants will need a variety of materials with which to present their own conclusions; the make-up of small groups may have to be decided; and the field study sessions and outside speakers have to be carefully prepared in advance. Each session, in fact, should be an example of good management.

The training guides mention overhead projectors and flip charts, and a video-recorder is suggested for one session, but none of this equipment is essential. All that is needed is a simple blackboard, and the training should emphasize simplicity rather than sophistication. Training of this kind should not take place in a luxurious and expensive environment. The whole focus of the course is on cost-effectiveness, and if the course itself involves unnecessary expense, this message will be lost. It should be difficult to forget the world of micro-enterprise with which the course is concerned, and it is far better to hold training courses of this type in a local community centre or village school than in a five-star hotel or international conference centre.

The enterprise experience

The course includes a number of sessions which together make up the 'enterprise experience', which provides the participants with an opportunity actually to start, manage and conclude a micro-enterprise, using their own money, during the course itself. This exercise has been successfully used with a large number of different participants, in courses in many different countries, and it has never failed to be a very valuable and at the same time an entertaining part of the course.

If the course is being run on a residential basis, over a continuous period, this component provides an invaluable thread through the programme, and the products and services offered by participants' individual enterprises can help to overcome many of the minor problems that people experience when they are 'stuck' in a possibly remote location, away from home, for an extended period.

It may be more difficult, however, to maintain the continuity and enthusiasm that this exercise needs if the course is held over a more extended period, with substantial breaks for return to work, and if the participants are not residing together for the duration of the course. In these circumstance it may be appropriate to omit the enterprise experience, and this can be done without seriously prejudicing other parts of the course.

The enterprise experience has been undertaken very many times, with NGO staff and others, in many different countries, and there has never been an occasion when all participants choose to run one single group enterprise together, although many of them seem to prefer other people to work in groups. In the unlikely event that they do all choose to work together, do not discourage them from this, and use the experience to draw conclusions about the special problems of group enterprises, and ways in which they can, or cannot, be solved.

The training itself

The book describes a complete ten and a half day course, divided into a total of 41 sessions, four to each day. If the course is being presented in this way, it will most likely be spread over two weeks, with a weekend in the middle, but the complete course may also take place over a far longer period, with sessions taking place only on certain days each week, or in the evenings or weekends.

Breaks of this kind will involve some loss of continuity, and such a course requires very careful planning and possibly some rearrangement of the order given in the book, but it will also have the advantage of enabling participants to relate the training to their work as it progresses, so that its practical value is continually reinforced.

The timings which are given for each session are also very approximate, and will vary depending on the level of the participants and the amount of detail which is covered. The discussions must be carefully controlled. It is important to elicit a wide range of views, and to be sure that less-confident participants also have a chance to contribute, and discussions must finish with some kind of consensus or at least a clear understanding of different points of view. It is far too easy to waste time discussing the exact meaning of words, instead of the practical implications. It is important to avoid this, and each of the many occasions devoted to discussion must be carefully monitored and guided so that a satisfactory conclusion is reached within the time available.

Evaluation

The course includes sessions on evaluation, and it focuses throughout on the necessity for NGOs to provide value for money in their work. In the interests of consistency, therefore, if for no other reason, training conducted with the use of this material must be properly evaluated. The third session on Day Nine covers evaluation, and uses the course itself as a simple case study; you should use this, as well as the third session on Day Ten, as a source of ideas as to how you can evaluate this, or indeed any enterprise development training. Participants should at the very minimum be asked at the end of each week, or preferably each day, to evaluate each session on a four-point scale such as: A = excellent, B = Good, C = So-so, D = A waste of time.

Some trainers, as well as some participants, may find the continuing emphasis on financial costs and benefits to be unfamiliar or even inappropriate. This training is about business, however, and business is about money. We once had a meeting for people who had attended our courses in the past, and one of them said that the main thing he had learned was that business development must itself be business-like; we hope that this manual will help a few more people to learn that lesson.

Introduction, our strengths, weaknesses and responsibilities

OBJECTIVE
To enable participants to identify their own and each other's strengths and weaknesses for effective enterprise development, and to maximize their commitment to the course.

TIME
One to one and a half hours.

NOTE Throughout this training guide, the words 'he' and 'she', 'him' and 'her', 'his' and 'hers' are to be taken as meaning female or male.

The word 'board' is used to mean chalkboard, whiteboard, overhead projector, flip chart or any other means you use to convey written information to participants. The use of the board is suggested at various stages but this does not of course mean that these are the only times it should be used. The instructor is advised to 'elicit' points from participants several times during most sessions. It is particularly important to give recognition to participants' suggestions by summarizing them on the board, using some of their own words whenever possible.

MATERIALS

Attitude survey hand-out: Prepare one copy per participant. This should if possible be given to the participants on arrival at the training place, with a request for them to complete it and hand in at registration or some time beforehand, to allow time for you to collate their answers. If this is not possible, the completed surveys should be handed to the instructor at the beginning of this first session.

'*Tick-list*': One copy for each participant of a list of the participants with a blank space for a written comment beside each name. This should also be given out to participants the day before this first session, with a note asking them each to find out any personal fact about each of their fellow participants, and to write it in the space provided. The purpose of this simple game is to get the participants to meet one another informally as quickly as possible, since each will have to speak to every other member individually in order to complete the exercise.

ADVANCE PREPARATION

Cost of the course: Make a very rough estimate of the total cost per participant of the course, as described in item 12 of the session guide. Do *not* give this figure to participants, or explain it in any way, since this would destroy the 'shock' element of the exercise.

SESSION GUIDE

1.   Introduce yourself and welcome the participants. Tell them the objective of the session, and, if it has not been possible to give them the attitude survey before, distribute it now and ask them to fill it in right away. Stress that they should give their opinions in relation to enterprise development or income generation for the poor.

If you have chosen to use the 'tick-list' game in order to break the ice, explain its purpose. You need not collect the completed papers, but ask one or two participants to read out intriguing facts they have discovered about one another in order to stress the informal nature of the whole course, which is enjoyable and is also essential for effective participative learning.

2.   Collect the completed survey papers. Explain that the whole approach of this course is participative. Ask participants what is different about sharing food or sharing knowledge with somebody else. Elicit the answer that if you share your food with someone, you have less to eat yourself, but if you share knowledge, your own knowledge is not diminished, and may even be improved through your effort to share it.

The sum of the experience and knowledge in the group is vast, and if everyone goes away with even a small part of the total, without any contribution from the instructor, an enormous amount will have been gained. Stress that your own task as instructor is mainly to facilitate this shared learning, and that everyone, including you, will learn from everyone else. It is therefore important to start by getting some idea of where we stand and what we need to learn. The attitude survey and the rest of this session are designed to help us do this.

3.   Explain that the course is also 'marketing oriented'. The participants are to think of themselves not as your students but as your *customers*, and you the instructor must satisfy them just like any business person must satisfy her customers if she is to remain in business, and just like any NGO employee must satisfy his clients if he is to do his job properly. This session is also designed to help you learn what the participants need.

4.   Divide the participants into pairs, as they are sitting; if there is an odd number of participants, you should yourself be a member of one pair. Ask the right-hand member of each pair to give the other, in no more than five minutes, the following information about himself. Stress that this information must relate to themselves, as individuals, and not to the strengths and weaknesses of their organizations as a

whole, or their superiors or subordinates. Warn them that everyone is going to have to tell the rest of the group about his/her partner, so they may want to take notes.

- Name, including the 'friendly' name by which he/she wishes to be known during the course.

- Organization.

- Job title, and what she/he *does*, since most titles, such as 'field co-ordinator', tell us very little about what people actually *do*.

- Some task in enterprise development he/she thinks they are good at. This might be a general skill such as communicating with people, encouraging people to work in groups or identifying business opportunities or it may be more specific like assessing business proposals, preparing accounts or actual selling.

- Similarly, some aspect of enterprise development she/he thinks they are weak or not so good at. Senior staff may find it difficult to share their weaknesses with their juniors. Help them to 'loosen up' by giving an example of a weakness of your own.

5. Ensure that these exchanges do not degenerate into general chat, and after at most five minutes ask participants to reverse roles.

6. Ask each participant to give the information she obtained about her partner to the rest of the group, in three minutes or less. This should be an exercise in concise presentation as well as an exchange of information.

While they are speaking, divide the board into two sections. Head one 'we are good at' and the other 'we are bad at' and write one-word summaries of each strength and weakness under the respective heading.

7. Do the same for the other members of each pair. If there is an even number of participants, present your own information yourself at the end. Be sure to make it clear that you have as much to learn as the participants. This will demonstrate the point you made in item 2 above.

8. When everyone's information has been given, draw lines across the board to link items that are some people's weaknesses to the same items that are other people's strengths. Show how this demonstrates the importance of sharing.

Some participants may have little or no experience of enterprise development, but be sure to elicit some strength even from those who are least confident, and to show that community development experience unrelated to enterprise, or recent full-time education, can also offer strengths to complement others who have more practical experience in the field of enterprise development.

9. Ask the participants to suggest definitions of the word 'enterprise'. This course is designed to help poor people to start and run them, so we need to be agreed what they are.

Participants may use phrases such as 'income-generating activities' or 'projects'; stress that the course is about **business**.

Business involves putting in money, materials and labour in order to get out more than you put in, that is, **profit**. Many NGO staff are nervous about words such as business and profit, because businesses have often tended to exploit and exclude the poor, rather than providing the means for the poor to improve their situation.

Stress that this need not be the case, and that enterprise development requires above all a 'businesslike' approach. Our aim is not to run away from business but to enable poor people to use the power of business enterprise on their own behalf, rather than being used by it.

Some participants may confuse 'entrepreneurship development' with 'enterprise development'. Stress that this course is about how to assist people to start and sustain their own enterprises, and how NGOs themselves can be more enterprising. Opinions differ about whether it is possible or necessary to train people to be entrepreneurial, but this course is about how to assist people who already want to be self-employed, probably because they have no alternative, to do so successfully.

10. Ask participants to describe a typical business of the kind that they wish to help poor people to develop. If participants describe a 'formal' business, which is registered, which employs several people and which may require several thousand dollars to start, ask them to describe something smaller. What is the smallest business they would consider to be worth encouraging?

Stress that even a woman who sells a few surplus bananas at the local market once a week, or a shoe shiner, are both business people. They are not being paid a regular wage, they are investing their own time, and perhaps some money too, in the hope that they will earn something more.

Most poor people's businesses are very small indeed, and might not usually be called businesses at all. It would be very good if all poor people could own or work in 'formal' small businesses but it is not possible. Most poor people must earn a living from very small 'informal' businesses, and NGOs must be willing and able to help them.

Official definitions of 'small' or 'micro' businesses usually define them in terms of a maximum amount of capital, or number of employees. During this course we shall generally ignore these upper limits, and concentrate on the really tiny businesses on which most poor people depend, and for which official definitions are irrelevant because they never receive any official assistance anyway.

11. Go through the timetable, relating individual sessions to the strengths and weaknesses that have been identified. Stress again that participants will be required to contribute, to calculate and generally to participate in the process of learning. They may disagree, even quite strongly, with some of the views expressed during the course, and they will have every opportunity to test their views against those of other members of the course and against international experience.

Stress that many participants will find some parts of the course difficult, and that they are responsible for 'quality control' by ensuring that you, the instructor, do your job properly. They must therefore stop you and ask questions whenever they do not understand, even if this makes them feel foolish.

Point out that the person who admits that he does not understand is not a fool. The real fool is the one who does *not* have the courage to admit that he does not understand. Any participant who asks for clarification can be sure that she is not alone; others will be grateful for her admission.

12. Before the session, make an estimate of the total cost of the course per participant, including the training and accommodation costs, transport to the train-

ing location, and for field visits. Include an approximate figure for the salary that each participant is being paid by her/his employer for the period of the course, since this is also a cost of the course, because participants are not doing their job while they are being trained. Their employers are 'investing' this time in the hope of future improved performance. 'Round' the figure down to the nearest hundred dollars, so that nobody can argue that it is an overestimate.

Do not at this point explain the figure to participants, but just ask each of them to think how this sum of money might best be spent on some form of income generation for their poor clients, and to make a very rough estimate of how many jobs this might create. Say that you are doing this in order to have some idea of the ways in which they believe jobs can be created.

Allow participants five minutes to think about this, and ask them to make a note, for their own reference only, of how the money might be spent, and the number of jobs.

13. Ask each participant quickly to state how she/he has suggested the money might be spent, and the number of jobs this would create. List these on the board, as briefly and as fast as possible. The answers will of course depend on the cost of the course and the views of the participants, but you may have a list rather like this:

How $1,000 might be spent to create jobs for the poor

Buy two welding machines	Four jobs
Train ten women in sewing	Five jobs
Set up one grocery shop	One job
(and so on)	

Write down the total of jobs which would be created.

14. Ask participants to suggest why you might have asked them to give you this information, apart from your initial explanation.

If they have no idea, ask them how much they think the course is costing for each of them. Elicit the conclusion that the cost is similar to the sum of money which you asked them to think about, and that the long list you have just written on the board, with the job-creation impact, represents an alternative way in which the money might have been spent.

15. If any of the participants have studied economics, ask one of them to explain to the others the concept of 'opportunity cost'. Show that this list and the jobs are in a very real sense the 'cost' of this course, in that the money could have been used to help people in these ways. What does this imply for the participants, and particularly for you the instructor?

Encourage the answer that the course will only be a good 'investment' if it results in more jobs being created than those you have listed. If it does not, it would have been better to spend the money in the ways participants just wrote down.

16. This exercise should have given the participants, and you yourself, something of a shock. Stress that you are all 'trustees' of the money that is being spent on the

11

course, on behalf of the poor people in whose service you are all employed. Unless the results of this course, measured in terms of job creation and income generation for poor people, are at least as impressive as the list on the board, it would have been better not to have the course at all.

You are all responsible for doing your best to achieve a better result, and it should be possible to do it. But it is not easy, since training courses so often fail actually to make any change in trainees' subsequent performance. This course is about business enterprise, which is about investing time and money in order to earn more money; the course itself, like participants' own day-to-day work, must be 'profitable' in terms not of the participants' income but increased income for poor people.

17. Conclude the session by asking the participants to comment on this first session, and to suggest ways in which the style, pace or method of instruction might be improved. Again, stress that they are your customers, as the poor people their NGOs serve are their customers. Check that all administrative arrangements such as food, accommodation or plans for transport home at the end of the course are satisfactory; if participants are worried about such things, they are unlikely to be able to concentrate on learning.

DAY ONE — SESSIONS ONE AND TWO

(Note: you need NOT write your name on this handout)

NGO ATTITUDE SURVEY

Below you will see ten statements relating to ways in which NGOs can help with the development of income-generating enterprise for the poor. Please read each statement, think briefly about it and indicate your opinion on that issue by putting a circle round the word 'agree', 'don't know' or 'disagree' in each case.

1. It is impossible to evaluate our work in enterprise development for the poor in terms of financial costs and benefits; human development cannot be valued in rupees and paise.

    Agree / Don't Know / Disagree

2. The best way to help poor people to increase their incomes is to help a few people, who may not themselves be poor, to develop enterprises which will employ the poor.

    Agree / Don't Know / Disagree

3. Poor people are unlikely to have their own good business ideas; NGOs must help them by giving them ideas.

    Agree / Don't Know / Disagree

4. Loans for poor people's businesses must be at lower than market interest rates or interest free.

    Agree / Don't Know / Disagree

5. NGOs should aim to charge the poor for enterprise development services, so that the NGOs themselves can become self-sustaining.

    Agree / Don't Know / Disagree

6. NGOs should always encourage poor people to start group or community owned enterprises, rather than individual businesses.

    Agree / Don't Know / Disagree

7. It is better to give grants to the poor to help them develop enterprises, rather than to make loans.

    Agree / Don't Know / Disagree

8. If we do make loans to the poor for enterprise development, we cannot expect them to repay them on time; we must be lenient.

    Agree / Don't Know / Disagree

9. Women are better at micro-enterprise than men; they re-invest the profits, or spend them on their families, and they repay loans better.

    Agree / Don't Know / Disagree

10. Most poor people do not need training to enable them to start a business; all they need is access to finance.

    Agree / Don't Know / Disagree

13

Our own views, and where do we stand now? The enterprise experience

OBJECTIVES

- *To enable participants to identify certain beliefs which are critical for effective enterprise development, and to recognize and, when appropriate, to question their own beliefs.*

- *To introduce participants to the 'enterprise experience'.*

TIME

One and a half to two hours.

MATERIALS

Hand-out; The enterprise experience, a list of the stages as given in item 10 in the session guide, together with clear times and dates for the various deadlines that are involved.

ADVANCE PREPARATION

If possible, go through the participants' completed attitude survey forms and add up the numbers who agree, disagree or do not know their view on each of the ten statements. Prepare a summary of the numbers, in the form shown under item 1 of the session guide.

NOTE In item 10 of the session guide, and later, reference is made to the 'bank' from which participants will be able to borrow money for their enterprise experiences. This 'bank' should be the training institution, and you, or a colleague, should be the manager. The maximum amount of money that will be needed is $10 per participant (or such larger sum as you may decide). This exercise has been conducted many times before, throughout the world, and it is most unusual for any participants actually to choose to take a loan, but it is important to offer the facility to avoid the complaint of shortage of capital. There have never been any defaults!

If, however, neither you, your institution nor anyone else is willing to take the small risk involved, the 'bank' facility may be omitted. It is possible that in such a case one or more participants will choose money-lending as their business.

SESSION GUIDE

1. Display the following list of statements on the board, to remind participants of the attitude survey:

	Agree	Don't know	Disagree
Financial evaluation is impossible			
Jobs for the poor, not self-employment			
We have to give the poor business ideas			
Charge the poor low interest or no interest			
Charge the poor fees for our services			
Always promote groups			
Grants are better than loans			
The poor cannot repay loans on time			
Women are better at micro-enterprise than men			
Most poor people don't need business training			

2. If you have been able to collate the answers before, write the numbers who agreed, or disagreed, or did not know, in the respective columns. Otherwise, ask participants to raise their hands to show what opinion they expressed, and write the numbers under the appropriate headings.

Some participants may argue that such issues cannot be generalized in this way, and that 'it depends' is the best answer, for some or all of the issues. They are right. There may be circumstances when every point of view is correct, but stress that this exercise is designed merely to draw out general attitudes, and to set the agenda for much of the rest of the course.

3. Ask a participant who has opted for the minority view on the first issue briefly to explain why, and then invite somebody who represents the majority view to argue for the other side. Do not allow general debate at this time, even though many partici-pants may have quite strong views for one side or the other on many of the ten issues.

If nobody or only a small number have opted for a particular point of view on any of the issues, it is even more important to bring out the arguments in favour of that view. If there are any such cases where participants' views are heavily one-sided, and if none of the participants is able to argue for the opposite view, you must yourself do this, even if you do not agree with it.

Experience world-wide shows that for most of these views, at least in most situations, there is a 'right' and a 'wrong' answer, although each situation must be treated on its merits. This course is about management, which is not about making or following rules but about learning to use independent judgement.

It is therefore vital to think through each of these issues, and to be aware of the arguments on each side, so that we can persuade others as well as being confident that we ourselves are 'right'.

4. Attempt to list, or if necessary yourself put forward, one or two reasons for each point of view. There are many other arguments, but some sample suggestions are as follows:

a. *Financial evaluation is impossible.*
   Agree: human welfare and dignity cannot be 'priced'; they are priceless.
   Disagree: business enterprise is about money; we are spending money in order to help people earn money; we must compare the two.

b. *Jobs for the poor, not self-employment.*
   Agree: the poor do not have the education, the skills or the contacts to start businesses; it is better for them to be employed by others who do have the resources.
   Disagree: when the poor are employed they are usually exploited; if they have their own businesses they will be genuinely 'empowered'.

c. *We have to give the poor business ideas.*
   Agree: the poor have not been exposed to business ideas, a primary function of outsiders is to show them what they can do.
   Disagree: the poor know their own situation better than we do; they know what their own resources are, and what they can produce or sell.

d. *Charge the poor low interest or no interest.*
   Agree: poverty means having little or no money, so it is self-evident that poor people cannot afford to pay a high price for money itself.
   Disagree: ready access to finance is more important for poor people than its price, high interest may be necessary to pay for this service.

e. *Charge the poor fees for our services.*
   Agree: people only value services if they have paid for them; free services are valued for what they cost, that is, nothing.
   Disagree: donors have given us their money to help poor people; we are breaking our trust if we sell services to the poor.

f. *Always promote groups.*
   Agree: poor people are always exploited by individual business people, even if they come from the same community. Strength comes from unity.
   Disagree: group enterprises have a bad record everywhere, they are more difficult to manage and they usually either fail or are 'hijacked'.

g. *Grants are better than loans.*
   Agree: the poor need every cent for survival, it is wrong to make them repay, and it costs more to administer the recovery than is recovered.
   Disagree: grants demean people and make them dependent on the donor.

h. *The poor cannot repay loans on time.*
   Agree: poor people are vulnerable to personal and natural disasters, they and their families will suffer if they are forced to repay.
   Disagree: if a loan has been correctly approved, the borrower should have no difficulty in repaying it on schedule.

i. *Women are better at micro-enterprise than men.*
   Agree: women always have to plan further ahead and to think of their children, men tend to spend any surplus on drink or other enjoyment.

Disagree: men are nearly always better educated than women, they understand money better and most successful big business owners are men.

j. *Most poor people don't need business training.*
Agree: success in micro-enterprise depends on shrewdness and local knowledge, not on things that can be taught on a course.
Disagree: people have no knowledge of business, particularly of record-keeping, they must be taught these things if they are to succeed.

5. Control the time carefully, since it is possible to spend a complete session or more discussing each of the issues; stress that the objective is to expose some of the critical issues, and to start participants thinking about them, rather than to have a full discussion.

6. Show that the traditional welfare-orientated NGO typically holds, or perhaps used to hold, the following views:

	Agree	Disagree
Financial evaluation is impossible	X	
Jobs for the poor, not self-employment		X
We have to give the poor business ideas	X	
Charge low interest or no interest	X	
Charge the poor fees for our services		X
Always promote groups	X	
Grants are better than loans	X	
The poor cannot repay loans on time	X	

People who hold the opposite views have generally been more successful in cost-effective enterprise development, but it is important that participants should form their own views; they may or may not change them as the course goes on.

7. Terminate the discussion; refer to the timetable, and show that the issues will each be dealt with in due time, not usually by general discussion but by reference to case-studies and participants' own field findings.

8. Ask any participant who knows how to ride a bicycle how she learned to do it. Encourage the answer that she learned by *doing*. At first she probably tried driving in a place where there were no other vehicles, and with guidance, but she did not learn by listening to lectures or reading books, she actually practised the skill by doing it.
   Ask participants what is the best way to learn anything. Encourage the discovery that the best way is by *doing*. We did not learn to speak our mother tongue, to read, to walk or to cook by being lectured about it, we learned by doing.

17

9. Ask if there is any participant who is now or ever in the past had experience of running his own business. There may be a few who have done this, but there are unlikely to be very many. Ask those who have not run their own businesses whether they learned to walk, to talk, to cook or to ride a bicycle from people who did not know how to do these things themselves; clearly not, we learn by watching and being taught by people who already have the skill we are acquiring.

Ask participants what this implies for their own efforts to help other people to run businesses; how can they help other people to do something they have never themselves done?

10. Explain that they are about to acquire this experience, during the course itself, on a small scale and in a brief period, but still in a real way. Each one of them, individually or in partnership with one or more others as he wishes, will:

- Identify a real business opportunity, here in the place where the course is being run.

- Carry out some simple 'research' into resources, markets and so on.

- Put together a simple business plan for the business.

- Invest her own money in the business, and, if she needs more money, apply for and if successful take a loan, with security, from a 'bank'.

- Run the business for ten days, including whatever production, marketing, selling and so on that are needed.

- Keep daily financial records for the business.

- At the end of the ten days, calculate the profit (or loss), repay any loan, distribute any profits and present the results to the rest of the group.

The owners of the business which made the most wages and profit for each of its owners, and those who keep the best records, will receive a small prize in recognition of their success.

11. Write the above stages of the 'enterprise experience', with the relevant dates and times, on the board. Ensure that every participant understands them, and distribute the hand-out including the deadline times and dates.

12. Some participants, particularly senior staff, may find it difficult to understand that they really are going to start and run little businesses during the course itself; they may think you are talking of case-studies or a simulation exercise.

Stress that it is 'for real'. They will be investing their own money, and providing some goods or services which other people, possibly their fellow participants, will buy with their own money because they are convinced that they need the service and that the price is worth paying.

Participants will have many questions. The following points will help to explain what is involved:

- They will have to think of their own ideas. You will not tell or even suggest to them what to do, but the next session may help them to identify business opportunities, as well as showing them how they in turn can help their clients to identify good ideas.

18

- Some participants may object that the training location is so remote or so poorly serviced that there are no opportunities. Stress that this means that there are many needs and few competitors.

- People have successfully taken part in this experience all over the world, even in as short a period as five days.

- They may choose to run individual businesses or to work with partners. It is up to them, but each participant should probably not be involved in more than one business, at least at the beginning.

- If they want to borrow money, they will have to convince the banker (who is you, the instructor) that their proposition is a good one, and they will have to deposit article(s) of value, such as a watch, some item of clothing or a book, which will be forfeit if the loan is not repaid. The bank will charge interest at one per cent per day, and the maximum loan will be $10 per person.

- Any profits they earn will be their property, and they will also have to bear any losses from their own pockets. This experience is designed not only to provide an opportunity to do the things that have to be done by whoever wants to start a business, but also to give participants the 'feel' of running a business, of risking their own money, persuading people to buy and so on.

13. Participants should begin now to think about what business to start, and whether to do it on their own or with partners. The next session will introduce them to some techniques for identifying business ideas.

How to generate business ideas

OBJECTIVE

To enable participants to identify business ideas for their 'enterprise experience' businesses, and also to help their own clients, when this is necessary, to generate business ideas for themselves.

TIME

One hour.

1. Remind participants of the third statement in the attitude questionnaire. We should not ourselves give poor people, or anyone else, ideas for businesses, but it *may* sometimes be useful to help them to identify business ideas for themselves. Ask participants why it is generally not advisable to give people ready-made business ideas.

In addition to whatever points that may have been made during the previous session, elicit arguments such as:

- If people start a business based on an idea they have been given by an NGO, which may also be lending them money to start it, they will blame the NGO if it fails, because, they will say, the NGO staff told them to start it.

- If someone has herself thought of her business idea, she will be determined to do her best to make it succeed, to prove her point. If it is somebody else's idea, the owner's commitment will be reduced.

- Most poor people have to run their businesses from their own homes, initially at any rate relying on local resources, local skills and the local market. They know far more about these things than any outsider ever can.

2. Ask participants individually to write down one minor problem which is affecting them right now, in the place where the training is taking place. Elicit suggestions such as:

- They are too hot, or too cold.

- The training institution is too far from the nearest shops and they forgot to bring some simple personal item such as soap, cigarettes or a towel.

- The institution is so isolated that the evenings are likely to be boring.

- They have not brought enough spending money with them.

- There is no way of communicating with home to tell their family that they arrived safely.

3. Summarize the problems on the board, and ask participants to suggest what this has got to do with identifying business opportunities. Elicit the answer that businesses are based on solving people's problems.

Ask participants to 'convert' each of the problems on the board into a business opportunity. Remind them that one definition of a good business person is that she is somebody who sees opportunities where other people see problems.

List participants' suggestions for business opportunities opposite each problem; examples to 'match' the above examples of problems might include:

- Start a shop to buy or rent warm clothes, heaters or blankets; or fans or air conditioners.

- Start a small campus-based shop, organize transport to the town, or offer a shopping service, for a small commission to be added to the cost of whatever is bought.

- Organize some evening entertainment, rent a video and show some films, organize a trip to the nearest cinema.

- Start a money-lending business or campus bank; borrow money from those who have some to spare, and lend it, at a higher rate of interest, to those who have not brought enough.

- Start a courier service; take letters to the post for a fee; organize a trip to the nearest public call office.

4. Show how the same principle applies to businesses that have sprung up everywhere in very large numbers in recent years; ask participants to suggest what businesses have grown out of the following problems:

- Educated young people cannot find employment (computer training schools).

- It takes a long time and is very expensive to get your own telephone line (private call offices).

- The post office is slow and unreliable (private fax services and inter-city couriers).

- Entrance to good schools is very difficult (private tutors).

5. Ask participants to suggest other ways of generating business ideas. Elicit possibilities such as:

- Applying existing skills to new products or services.

- Using available materials for different products.

- Finding new uses for existing products.

Ask participants to identify examples of local businesses which exemplify these approaches to idea generation, and stress that the search for business ideas requires self-confidence and optimism. We are all inclined to look for negative reasons why something can*not* be done, rather than to be positive and optimistic. The following exercise is designed to force us to 'think positively'.

Ask a participant who said earlier in the session that he does have a real business, or, if nobody has, any participant who has been putting forward ideas earlier in this session, to tell the class something about his real business, or one that he imagines he might start. In particular, he should identify some of the problems that are now or

21

might in the future be facing him. If none of the participants are willing to do this, you must do it yourself.

Tell the other participants that they must come up with POSITIVE suggestions as to how each of the problems might be exploited in order to improve the business. Encourage everyone to put forward ideas, no matter how wild or apparently ridiculous; the only two rules are:

- Every suggestion must be positive.

- Nobody is allowed to criticize anybody else's ideas, only to add to them so that they are even more forward-looking.

6. Encourage a free flow of 'wild' ideas, if necessary by putting some forward yourself. Some examples might be:

Problem: there is a shortage of cooking oil.
Solution: start growing oil seeds and pressing oil yourself.

Problem: I cannot identify a suitably skilled worker.
Solution: start a skills training school.

Problem: I have no capital, and my workers will steal all my money.
Solution: get the workers to be shareholders in the business.

Problem: there is a shortage of raw material.
Solution: hire unemployed youths to collect scrap material.

Problem: my potential customers all need credit.
Solution: start a bank and lend them money.

All these solutions have actually been implemented by business people who faced these problems.

7. Many if not most of the ideas generated by this 'brainstorming' approach may seem unrealistic or even stupid, but ask participants how their own grandparents or great-grandparents might have reacted 60 years ago to suggestions such as:

- A machine to carry 500 people half-way around the world in twelve hours.

- A small typewriter without paper which could store hundreds of pages of writing or other information and allow it to be printed or changed at any time.

- A little piece of plastic which could be used instead of money, all over the world.

- A small box with a glass screen on the front which could show people things that were happening anywhere in the world, as they were happening.

The people who invented and then built businesses on these apparently mad ideas were not fools. They were optimists who realized that they could satisfy people's needs for more rapid travel, for easier typing and access to data, for making payments without cash and for home-based information and entertainment, by matching them to new technology.

Ask participants what motivated the people who built businesses on these needs and ideas, and who continue to do the same all over the world. Were they motivated by a desire to serve their fellow human beings, by technical curiosity, or what?

Like all people who start businesses, they wanted to make a *profit*, to compensate them for the risks they took and for their hard work; many famous business pioneers, like so many of the thousands of more modest innovators who start businesses every day, failed and lost all their money. Others succeeded and became millionaires, but the needs which they identified would never have been satisfied if these people had not been willing to take the optimistic view and risk their money and their labour.

8. Business involves more than optimism. It also requires some simple planning. If the person starting the business wants to borrow money from other people to add to her own money, she will also have to persuade the other people that the business is a good possibility. This requires a business plan, which is the subject of the next session.

Planning for business

OBJECTIVE

To enable participants to identify the critical information that is needed to plan a new business, and to organize this information into a form which will facilitate rapid appraisal by the business owner herself or by others.

TIME

One to one and a half hours.

ADVANCE PREPARATION

If possible, every participant should by this session have selected his business idea for the enterprise experience, and should also have decided whether to work alone or with others, and, if the latter, the partnerships should be settled.

SESSION GUIDE

1. Ask participants what bankers usually ask people to produce before they will consider approving a loan for a new business venture. Elicit the answer that they require a 'feasibility study' or a 'project proposal'. Ask any participants who are familiar with such documents briefly to describe a typical study of this kind.

2. Ask participants what are the main differences between the 'formal' small businesses that are the subject of such studies and most poor people's businesses; why do poor people not prepare feasibility studies for their businesses?

- Very few poor people apply for bank loans for their businesses, because bankers are not willing to lend very small amounts to people without security.

- The cost of writing such a study may exceed the total amount of capital needed for a micro-business.

- Micro-business people, and particularly women, usually have neither the time nor the education to produce such studies.

3. Ask participants whether this means that there is no need to do any planning for a micro-enterprise, such as the ones they are about to start for their enterprise experiences, or the businesses operated by their clients.

Many 'formal' feasibility studies or business plans are prepared only because bankers demand them, and many such studies are actually prepared by consultants and the actual business owners neither know nor care about the details, but only about getting the loan. It is nevertheless useful for anyone who plans to start a business, even if she does not need a loan, to go through the planning process, even if not in writing.

Anyone who plans to start any business, however small, needs to ask and find the answers to a number of questions. The format of a formal feasibility study, properly simplified, can provide a useful guide for this. This is why participants are going to have to prepare plans for their enterprise experience businesses.

4. Ask participants to imagine that a client of their NGO has approached them to ask for advice about starting a business. They should write down the critical questions that they would ask such a person, in order to help her decide whether and how to start it.

Allow five minutes for this. Then go round the class asking each participant to suggest *one* item. In this and similar exercises, do not allow one participant to monopolize the learning process by giving all the answers; ensure that the less 'pushy' participants also have a chance to contribute their suggestion, and that their ideas are also recognized.

5. Summarize the suggestions on the board. Do not write down the same item twice when it is expressed in different words, but do include every separate suggestion, even if it does not appear useful.

It is likely that participants will have included several questions which cannot be answered, or whose answers would cost far more to obtain than the information is worth. Examples of such questions might be:

- Exactly how many people visit the market at X each day?

- What will be the cost of receipt books?

Remind participants that:

- Nobody can predict the future, all we can do is make informed guesses as to what may happen.

- It is not worth spending a great deal of money, or time, which costs money, to obtain information which is not worth very much. Getting information is like training; it is an investment which must be judged against the value of what is obtained.

6. Eliminate questions which do not seem either to be answerable or worth asking. Ensure that the surviving questions include at least the following, and elicit any missing questions if necessary.

a. What product or service is the business going to provide?

b. Who will be the customers, and why will they buy from this business rather than from its competitors?

c. What important equipment or materials and supplies will be needed, where and when will they be obtained, and how much will they cost?

d. Who is starting the business, and what skills and experience does she have which should enable her to succeed?

e. What is the best guess of the total revenue, costs and resulting profit or loss during the first month, year or whatever period is relevant? When is the business expected to be profitable?

f. How much money is needed to set up the business and keep it going until it starts to make a profit?

g. Who is going to provide this money? If it will have to be borrowed, when can it be paid back, and what security will the lender have?

Ensure that the main stress is on the customers and the demand for the products or services of the proposed business. Too many business plans are prepared on the assumption that whatever can be produced will be sold. This has never been true for micro-enterprises, and is ceasing to be true for larger public- and private-sector businesses as the market becomes more competitive.

7. You need not use these exact words, and some items may be subdivided into two or more questions if this is how participants have expressed them. It is important not to suggest any standard format for business planning, since this can easily degenerate into a mechanical formal exercise. Use simple non-jargon words, however, and point out to participants that although terms like 'marketing research', 'cash flow' or 'investment capital' are not used, the day-to-day words mean the same thing.
    Stress here and throughout the course that participants who are familiar with such terms should 'un-learn' them, and those who have not heard of them are fortunate. When we are dealing with poor and uneducated people we must speak in words they understand, and the effort to do this should help us to understand better what we are talking about.

8. Refer to the earlier discussion where it was shown that even an illiterate person starting a very small business can usefully go through such a planning exercise.
    Ask participants to test this assertion. Ask a volunteer to put herself in the position of somebody she knows who runs a very small business, such as a village woman who sells fruit in the market, or a shoe shiner.

- How might this person have answered these questions before starting the business?

- Would the exercise have been of any value, might it have helped to avoid mistakes or to reveal how the business might have been made more profitable?

9. Elicit further examples where such a check-list might have helped:

- Most people copy other businesses rather than trying to offer something different. Question (b) might lead to ideas for better packaging or products or a better location to attract customers.

- A business has to be based on a good idea, but the person who works in the business should also have some particular skill or experience to make it succeed; this is not likely to be an academic qualification, but may be a domestic skill, a hobby interest or some working experience. Asking question (d) can help to identify this ability, or its absence.

- Many businesses fail not because they are unprofitable, but because their owners have not put in enough money at the beginning to keep the business going until it makes a profit. The answer to question (f) will help to avoid this problem, or will show that the business cannot be started with the available money.

Stress that the decision *not* to start a business may be a very good decision. Refer to the previous session. You have to be an optimist to generate good business ideas, but you have to be a realist to avoid starting a business that has little hope of succeeding. A business plan can help optimists to be realists.

10. Remind participants that they must now prepare business plans for their enterprise experience businesses according to the agreed format.

They must also make a presentation of their business plan to the rest of the group tomorrow. The owners of a partnership business must agree on who will make the presentation, and each business will be allowed a maximum of five minutes for its presentation.

If possible, participants should be given newsprint sheets and markers, or overhead transparency sheets and pens, to prepare visual aids to support their presentations. Stress that this will be an opportunity not only to learn about business planning but also to practise the vital and often neglected skill of communicating a great deal of information to a group of people in a short period. Successful enterprise development, like running an actual business, depends on good communication.

Briefly go through some of the basic principles of presentation:

- Any visual aids must be neat, and the written words should be clear, legible and cover summary points only.

- The sequence must be logical and clear.

- The figures must be clear, neatly written and correctly calculated.

- Responsibilities within any group businesses must be agreed before the actual presentations.

- The enterprise experience is intended to be good fun, but it is also a serious learning exercise. Presenters must be well-prepared and confident.

Ensure that everyone has copied the final list so that no important items are omitted, and stress that every participant must have a business to present for the next session, whether as an individual or as a member of a group business.

Business plan presentations

OBJECTIVE   *To enable participants to present their enterprise experi-ence plans and thus to improve their presentation skills and their ability to assist their clients to plan their own businesses.*

TIME   *Approximately ten minutes per 'business', plus about half an hour.*

MATERIALS

The 'bank' will need a small supply of loan agreement forms, which should be drawn up formally, and should include:

- The name(s) of the borrower(s) and their business, and of the bank manager.

- The date(s) and times by when the loan is agreed to be repaid (all loans must be repaid before the final presentations of results in Day Nine — Session One).

- A brief description of the security which has been taken, and a statement that the borrowers agree that it may be retained until complete repayment has been made, or, if the lender so wishes, it may be sold to cover the debt, and that any surplus will be returned to the borrowers.

- Duly dated and witnessed signatures of the borrower(s) and the 'bank manager'.

SESSION GUIDE

1. If you do not already have this information, ask participants to state what business each proposes to start. List the businesses and their owners on the board. There may still be some misunderstandings or uncertainties, since they have not had very much time. Some participants may, if they wish, be involved in more than one business, but every participant must be involved in at least one.

Remind participants that each business is allowed five minutes only for its presentation. Enforce this rigidly, by warning presenters when they have taken four minutes, and stopping them after five.

2. Choose one business to start, and nominate one other participant to comment on the actual presentation itself and another to comment on the content. Stress the distinction between presentation and content. NGOs often fail to obtain funding or other support not because the content of their plans is poor but because they fail to present them properly. The commentators' comments should be invited after the presentation, and should be used to initiate discussion for about five minutes, before the next business is presented by its owner(s).

Suggest that the commentators on the presentations might focus their attention on aspects such as:

- The clarity and legibility of any visual aids.

- The logical sequence of the presentation.

- The confidence and knowledge of the presenter(s).

The content commentators should focus on questions such as:

- Were the figures correctly calculated and reasonable?

- Was all the information relevant, and were any important items omitted?

- Is the business convincing, would the commentator herself invest her own money in it?

Write both sets of questions on flip-chart sheets and display them in the classroom. They will be useful in this and in later sessions when participants have to make presentations.

Invite other participants to comment further after each nominated commentator has shared his views. Remind them of Session Three, and of the need for optimism. These presentations relate not only to the enterprise experience, but they also provide an opportunity to develop the ability to make rapid business assessments, and to make positive and constructive comments and suggestions. This is a vital task in the job of enterprise development.

In this and several later sessions it is suggested that participants should be asked to comment on one another's presentations; it is important to elicit as many comments as possible from participants, but you yourself should also add any important points which they have missed.

In particular, be sure to correct any mathematical or other basic errors which have not been mentioned by the commentators or other participants. In particular, ask any participants who criticized presentations for missing information to state *how* they would suggest the information might have been obtained.

Most business plans neglect the question '*Why* should people buy my goods or services?' Their writers assume that because the business exists people will buy from it. Ensure that this point is properly covered.

3. Continue through all the businesses in the same way; in this and subsequent sessions when participants are being asked to make presentations, avoid following a preset sequence, such as going round the training room from left to right. If your choices are unexpected, participants will not be so tempted to relax because they know that they have a long wait before their turn.

Nominate different 'commentators' for each business, and ensure that every participant is nominated at least once. Participants who are shy or lack confidence must be encouraged to take their turn in this way.

4. These presentations will have revealed that some businesses will be quite profitable, and it is likely that most participants have aimed their businesses at the 'market' of their fellow participants. Some participants may object. Point out that they will be free to buy or not, and indeed to offer the same goods or services at a lower price in competition if they wish. People who start businesses deserve a reward for the risk and the idea.

29

There may also be more than one business offering the same services, such as laundry, or transport. Even if this has not happened, ask participants to imagine how they might have felt if someone else had proposed to start an identical business to theirs.

Some might be inclined to give up, because they have lost what they thought was their monopoly. Remind them of the reality of every village market, where there are large numbers of businesses offering the same goods. Point out that subsequent sessions on marketing will deal in more detail with marketing, but ask participants how so many apparently similar businesses do survive, and how some prosper and some disappear. Is there indeed any real monopoly business, apart from government-imposed ones, which are fast disappearing?

Elicit the suggestion that successful business owners try to make their businesses different from their competitors, even in very modest ways. They may be more friendly to their customers, they may stay open longer, they may deliver their goods or services right to people's houses. The enterprise experience provides an opportunity to practise marketing skills of this sort.

5. It is still possible that some participants might want to make radical changes in their businesses, after presenting their plans. Clarify that their business plans do not oblige them in any way actually to start the businesses they have described, and to work towards the results they have forecast.

One of the strengths of small businesses is that the people who own them can rapidly adapt them or even change them completely in response to new challenges and new opportunities. Participants, like their clients, are free to change their plans at any time if they wish. Business plans are like a map, which shows the way but does not force the traveller to follow it if he decides to go somewhere different.

6. Tell participants that they should now start their businesses. Some indeed may have already started, and this is quite acceptable. Remind them that they will have to keep records of all the money that comes into and goes out of their businesses, whether it comes from the owners or from the customers, and whether it is used for paying wages, for buying supplies or any other purpose.

Remind them that one of the major problems of small business owners is that they fail to distinguish between their personal money and that which belongs to the business. Even if you are the only owner of a business, you must keep its money separate from your own, and carefully control the amount of money (or goods) you take out of it (or put into it). The enterprise experience is a good exercise in this separation task. Participants may choose to pay themselves wages for their labour, or they may prefer to accumulate the profit (if any) and to pay themselves by distributing it at the end. It is up to them.

7. Stress in conclusion that participants should try to remember that the enterprise experience is not primarily a way for them to try to make some profit, nor a way of providing services and entertainment during the course, but it is a way of learning about business enterprise by being enterprising and businesslike. They should run their businesses enthusiastically, but should at the same time try to think about their own experience and learn from it how they can help their clients more effectively.

NOTE After the session, invite any participants who want to borrow money to meet you individually. Ask them to present their case for a loan to you, and be critical, like any sceptical bank manager. They must be able to show you why they are confident they can repay as they propose, and if you are not convinced you should ask them to improve their case and come to see you again later.

Ensure that they have correctly calculated the interest payments in accordance with the amount of loan that will be outstanding each day. Appraise the security, and be sure that it is something of value to the borrowers, even if its resale value might not cover the full amount of the loan. A cheque book, a credit card, some books or an identity card are all appropriate. If you are satisfied, conclude the meeting by completing the loan agreement form, taking the security and handing over the cash.

The financial reality of an enterprise

OBJECTIVE

To enable participants to describe the sources and forms in which money is being used in a business, and the operating results, in the form of a simple 'balance sheet' and 'profit-and-loss statement', and to use and explain these statements without employing technical accounting terms.

TIME

One and a half to two hours.

ADVANCE PREPARATION

It is not necessary, or desirable, to have a qualified accountant to handle this and other sessions which deal with financial figures, since the participants will learn more effectively if they feel they are learning with rather than from the instructor. It is nevertheless particularly important that the instructor should be well prepared for these sessions. It may also be useful to ask people who are familiar with local languages how they would translate accounting terminology.

SESSION GUIDE

1. Remind participants of the first session, when they described what they did at work, and identified their strengths and their weaknesses in the field of enterprise development. Some will almost certainly have identified accounts already as a weak area, and some may also have said that this was an area where they were strong.

In this and the following sessions, both will learn. Those who have some experience of financial accounting will learn how to apply their knowledge to the reality of the very smallest businesses owned by poor people. Others who know little or nothing now will by the end of the day be able to use simple accounts in a very practical way.

Those who have some knowledge may also have to 'unlearn', since much of what we learn in accounting is made unnecessarily complicated by unfamiliar words. As we shall see, the basic concepts of accounts are straightforward and very useful, even for the smallest businesses and for illiterate people.

Some of the material will be very familiar to participants who have accounting experience. They can still learn a great deal about how to explain and use accounting tools to communicate with people who have no such experience. They should act as 'consultants' to their fellow participants who know less of accounts, but they must *not* just give the answers, since people learn not from being told but from being helped to discover for themselves.

2. Write the following words on the board:

Balance sheet	*Debtors*
Creditors	*Liabilities*
Reserves	*Depreciation*

(If the course is being conducted in a language which has its own words for these accounting terms, write the 'formal' words which are used by educated people in the area.)

Ask participants to write down translations of these words in a local language which is spoken by many of their poorest clients. This may be a tribal or a regional language. They should not at this stage discuss their efforts with their neighbours.

Participants may have difficulty, either because they do not know what the words mean in English or because it is difficult to express their meaning in vernacular languages. Tell them to do their best, the very difficulty of the task is the main lesson.

3. Allow about five minutes for this translation. Then ask each participant to exchange his paper with another participant, who has some knowledge of the language that has been used. Ask some participants to translate what has been written literally back into English, or whatever language the course is being conducted in, without using their prior knowledge of the meaning of the original words.

The results will probably be confusing and perhaps meaningless or even quite contrary to the meaning of the original accounting terms. Point out that this shows how difficult it is to communicate with our clients if we try to work with the 'jargon' words which accountants normally use. The object of this session is to see how basic and practical the underlying tools of accounting really are.

Ask if any participant has recently taken a prescription from a doctor. Could she read and understand it herself?

Usually doctors write prescriptions illegibly and using words that ordinary people cannot understand. Like all 'professionals', such as lawyers, priests, engineers and accountants, they wish to preserve the mystery of their craft. Our objective is to break through the mysteries of accounting, and to help our clients to break through them, so that we and they can use the tools ourselves.

4. Ask a participant who has some knowledge of accounts to explain to the rest of the class, in everyday words such as can be understood by somebody who has no knowledge of accounting, what each of the six terms means.

Stress that the precise definitions do not matter. What is important is that participants, and their clients, should understand and be able to use the practical accounting tools that the technical terms so often prevent ordinary people from using.

They should say something along the lines of:

- *Balance sheet*: A description of the financial position of a business showing where the money has come from and how it is being used at a particular point of time.

- *Debtors*: The amount of money that is owed to a business by its customers.

- *Creditors*: The amount of money that is owed by a business to its suppliers.

- *Depreciation*: The reduction in value of equipment that results from its being used.

33

- *Reserves*:   The money that has been reinvested in the business out of its profits.

- *Liabilities*:   The sources from which the money in a business has come.

Ask participants who have no prior knowledge of accounting to suggest simple words that we can use in this and subsequent sessions, in place of confusing words such as 'debtors' and 'creditors' whose meanings we can only remember if we learn them by heart.

Encourage participants to suggest and agree on their own terms, possibly in local languages, and use them in subsequent sessions. In this material we shall hereafter use the following terms, the first four of which are the words used by American accountants, which are generally less mysterious than the English terms:

Balance sheet:	'Statement of condition'.
Debtors:	'Accounts receivable'.
Trading account:	'Operating statement'.
Creditors:	'Accounts payable'.
Depreciation:	'Value reduction'.
Reserves:	'Retained earnings'.
Assets:	'Uses' or 'what the business owns'.
Liabilities:	'sources'.

5. Explain that participants will now produce accounts for several real businesses, starting with some of their own enterprise experience businesses. Ask if any of them are familiar with moving picture film, which is made up of large numbers of 'still' pictures which when run together produce the moving pictures we see at a cinema.

Sketch a strip of film on the board, and ask what an individual 'still' shows. It is a picture of the scene at one instant of time, which we can study at leisure to see all the details. Ask what the film shows when it is run together. We lose the individual detail, but we can see what happens over a period of time. Can participants relate this to financial accounts? Explain that the 'balance sheet' or statement of condition is like a single 'still'; it shows the financial position at a moment of time. Accountants usually produce these statements at the end of a financial year, but we can, and indeed will, produce them for any moment in the life of a business.

A trading or profit-and-loss account, or as we shall call it an operating statement, is like a movie; it shows what has happened over a period, which may be a year but may also be a month, a week or a day. The period should be chosen according to the nature of the business and the use for which the statement is intended, not because of any accounting conventions.

6. Identify a participant who is running her enterprise experience on her own, who has not taken a 'bank' loan for it, and, if possible, has no previous knowledge of accounting.

Ask her to describe the financial position of her enterprise, at the moment (which may be now), when she had already put some of her money into it but had not yet spent any of the money. From the point of view of the business, what was the source of its money, and in what form is it now owned by the business?

Do not allow participants who are familiar with accounts to answer. Encourage the following answers and write the 'statement of condition' of the participant's business on the board as follows, of course using the correct figure:

34

Uses ($)		Sources ($)	
Cash	10	The owner	10

Ask a participant who does know something of accounts to say what this statement is; it is a balance sheet for the business at that moment. Stress that the words, the layout and the sequence which are used are unimportant, and professional accountants in fact use many different layouts according to the way they were trained. What matters is that every participant understands what the figures mean.

7. Ask a partner in another enterprise experience, preferably one which has more than one owner and which has already bought or received from the owners some equipment or materials, so that it owns something in addition to cash, to do the same for his business.

As before, do not allow participants with accounting knowledge to answer, and elicit the figures in the following form (the following figures might be for a laundry business):

Uses ($)		Sources ($)	
Cash	5	Owner A, cash	10
Soap powder	4	Owner B, bowl worth	10
Washing bowl	10		
Notebook	1		
Total	20	Total	20

Explain that this statement is called a 'balance sheet' because the total figures 'balance', that is, they are the same. There is no mystery in this, since the two columns are merely giving different information about the same sum of money: how it is being used in the business and where it came from.

8. Ask another participant who presented a simple and reasonable forecast of the results of his enterprise experience business to repeat the figures. Write them on the board in the following form:

		$
Sales		100
Cost of items sold		70
Difference		30
Expenses:		
Poster	2	
Wages	18	
Total Expenses		20
Profit		10

As before, ask a participant with accounting experience to say what this statement is: it is a profit-and-loss account or statement of operations, or rather a forecast of such a statement, for a certain specified period.

As with the statement of condition, stress that the details of the layout are not important. It is not always necessary to show the margin between the sales revenue and the cost of what was sold, for instance, particularly when the business is a laundry, a barber, a shoe shiner or other service business where little or no materials are consumed directly for each sale.

In trading businesses, however, where the main expense is the goods which are bought and sold, this margin is obviously an important figure. Participants may be more familiar with the phrase 'gross profit'. Here again, stress that the words are not important. What matters is the use to which the figures will be put.

9. Refer back to the simple statement of condition or balance sheet produced in item 7 above. In this example, the things owned by the business included materials (the washing powder in our example) and equipment (the bowl). Ask participants what other ways there are in which money can be owned by a business, apart from cash, materials and equipment?

Elicit answers such as the following. As before, do not allow accountants to answer, and elicit any items that may have been omitted by asking questions rather than merely giving the missing item yourself:

- Bank balances.

- Money owed by customers for goods taken on credit (the right to receive the money in the future, as represented perhaps by an IOU, is something that can be owned. Point out that cheques, and even bank notes, are really the same thing).

- Partly finished goods.

- Buildings.

- Advance payments (some businesses have to pay in advance for rent, electricity or other services; if they have not yet 'used up' what they have paid for, the right to use it is something that the business owns).

10. Refer again to the same statement of condition, but to the 'sources' side. The two owners were the only sources of money for this business. Ask participants what other sources of money there are. As before, make a list that includes the following items:

- Bank loans.

- Money owed to suppliers for supplies taken on credit.

- Advance deposits from customers (these are the same as loans, since the business owes the customer the money until the product has been delivered).

- Profits that have not been taken out by the owners, but have been retained in the business.

Participants may suggest sales as a source of money. They are of course right, in that sales revenue is the main way in which a business gets money, once it has started operations.

Stress, however, that the 'still' picture only includes what is in the business at that moment of time; the money indeed came in from sales, but most of it probably went out in the form of labour, materials and so on. The still picture only includes what remains, if anything, which is that part of the profits that has not been withdrawn by the owner(s).

11. Ask participants each to recall a very small business owned by one of their clients or somebody with whom they are very familiar, preferably a straightforward trading business such as a fruit or vegetable vendor.

Choose one participant. Ask her first briefly to describe the business she has recalled, without mentioning figures. Then ask the other participants in turn each to ask her for one figure. Draw up a layout and write the figures she gives in answer on the board as the participant who asked the question directs you.

The business for which the figures are being obtained probably has no written records. Ask the participant who is familiar with it to make the best guesses she can, and to admit that she has no idea when that is the case.

Go round the class until every relevant figure has been requested. Ensure that participants remember to ask whether the business sells or buys on credit, whether it has a bank account, whether any customers pay in advance, and so on. They will be repeating this exercise later in the course in the field, with real businesses, and they will only be able to get complete information if they remember to ask for every item.

12. Very few of the owners of the sort of businesses with which we are dealing know how much profit (or loss) they are making, and even fewer make a conscious decision to withdraw, or leave in the business, a certain proportion of the profits. If participants have asked how much money the owner has reinvested in the business from the profits, the participant who is familiar with the business is most unlikely to have been able to give an answer.

The total figures for the way money is being used, and the sources, are therefore unlikely to balance. Ask participants to explain the difference, and if necessary write on the board some hypothetical figures such as the following:

Uses ($)		Sources ($)	
Cash	15	Owner A, cash	10
Soap powder	4	Owner B, bowl worth	10
Washing bowl	10	Loan from 'bank'	5
Notebook	1		
Owed by customer	5		
Total	35	Total	25

Elicit the answer that if the figures for the ways in which money is being used and the sources are complete and correct, the only possible source of the difference is retained earnings; the owners have, probably without being aware of it, left $10 in the business from its profits.

The corrected statement of condition should therefore read:

Uses ($)		Sources ($)	
Cash	15	Owner A, cash	10
Soap powder	4	Owner B, bowl worth	10
Washing bowl	10	Loan from 'bank'	5
Notebook	1	Retained profits	10
Owed by customer	5		
Total	35	Total	35

13. Amend the figures so that the total of 'uses' is less than the total of the 'sources', as in the following example. Ask participants to explain what is missing in such a case:

Uses ($)		Sources ($)	
Cash	15	Owner A, cash	10
Soap powder	4	Owner B, bowl worth	10
Washing bowl	10	Loan from 'bank'	20
Notebook	1		
Total	30	Total	40

In this case, more money has come into the business from the sources than is represented by the ways in which it is now being used. As in the previous example, if the figures are complete and correct, the only explanation is that the business has lost money. The statement of condition should be corrected as follows:

Uses ($)		Sources ($)	
Cash	15	Owner A, cash	10
Soap powder	4	Owner B, bowl worth	10
Washing bowl	10	Loan from 'bank'	20
Notebook	1	*Less* losses	(10)
Total	30	Total	30

Participants may find it clearer to add the amount of losses to the uses side, rather than subtracting it from the sources. Either is correct, what is important is that they should understand the principle.

14. Ensure that at this and every stage all participants, and not only those who have already had accounting experience, understand each stage.

Many of the concepts are difficult to grasp at first, and a great deal has been covered in this session. Ask those participants who do understand further to develop their understanding, and, what is even more important for NGO workers, their ability to share their understanding, by explaining difficult points to those who have difficulty.

This provides an opportunity for you, the instructor, to demonstrate your commitment to mutual learning and your commitment to full participation. Encourage participants themselves to try to explain to the others points that you yourself have failed to put across, and stress that you are all learning practical accounting and the far more difficult and important skills of communicating with your colleagues and your clients.

The 'dynamic balance sheet'

OBJECTIVE   *To enable participants to apply, expand and test what they have learned so far about simple accounts, in order to be able to elicit simple figures from real businesses.*

TIME   *Two to three hours.*

ADVANCE PREPARATION

It is of course vital that the instructor should be fully prepared for every session; this session is particularly demanding, however, and you should not only read through it carefully and make sure you understand every step but you should also be ready for participants to ask you how to deal with other types of transactions, which may not be included in this example. You may also have to allow time for individual discussions with some participants after the session.

SESSION GUIDE

1. Warn participants that they are now to have an opportunity to test what they have learned in the previous session, and to identify and fill any gaps. Stress that neither this not any other part of the course is an 'examination' or test in the sense of which they are probably accustomed. The purpose of our tests is to find out for ourselves what further we need to learn, and the only person whose skill is being tested in the traditional way is you, the instructor.

2. Refer back to the simple 'still picture' of the very first stage of a participant's enterprise experience business which was produced in item 6 of the last session. In order to keep the exercise simple, this should be a simple trading business, with no processing or manufacturing involved. Write the same figures on the board again (or work from the figures given in this session guide if you prefer).

Uses ($)		Sources ($)	
Cash	10	The owner	10
Total	10	Total	10

Ask a participant to suggest what might be the next transaction in this business. Stress that the transactions which he and subsequent participants suggest need not be realistic or carefully thought out. The objective is to try to see how all kinds of transactions affect the financial condition.

3. The next transaction is:

The business buys $6 worth of goods for cash, for resale. Note that we refer to 'the business' rather than 'the owner', in order to stress that the figures relate to the business as a separate entity from the person who owns it. Ask how the statement of condition should be changed; try to get the following answer:

	Uses ($)		Sources ($)
Cash	4	The owner	10
Stocks	6		
Total	10	Total	10

Stress that the total amount of money in the business has not changed; the only difference is in the way it is being used.

4. Go round the class, asking each participant in turn to suggest a transaction and to say how the figures should be changed. In the session guide, we shall simply show suggested transactions followed by the revised figures and any special points regarding that entry.
   The business sells for $4 in cash goods which cost $3.

	Uses ($)		Sources ($)
Cash	8	The owner	10
Stocks	3	Profits	1
Total	11	Total	11

The business now owns $1 more than it did before, and the source of this new money is the profit made on the sale.

41

5. The business puts $2 into a bank savings account.

Uses ($)		Sources ($)	
Cash	6	The owner	10
Bank account	2		
Stocks	3	Profits	1
Total	11	Total	11

6. The business sells goods which cost $2 for $3, on credit.

Uses ($)		Sources ($)	
Cash	6	The owner	10
Bank account	2		
Stocks	1	Profits	2
Owed to business	3		
Total	12	Total	12

The debt owed by the customer, that is the right to receive the money in the future, is 'owned' by the business.

7. The business buys $5 worth of new stocks, for cash.

Uses ($)		Sources ($)	
Cash	1	The owner	10
Bank account	2		
Stocks	6	Profits	2
Owed to business	3		
Total	12	Total	12

8. The credit customer pays $2 of her debt, in cash.

Uses ($)		Sources ($)	
Cash	3	The owner	10
Bank account	2		
Stocks	6	Profits	2
Owed to business	1		
Total	12	Total	12

The total amount of money in the business has not changed, since the profit was made when the goods were sold, not when they were paid for.

9. The owner takes $1 cash out of the business for her own use.

Uses ($)		Sources ($)	
Cash	2	The owner	10
Bank account	2		
Stocks	6	Profits	1
Owed to business	1		
Total	11	Total	11

The source figure for profits has gone down by $1. It does not matter whether this withdrawal by the owner is called 'wages' or 'drawings'; the effect on the figures, and on the financial position of the business, is the same.

10. The business buys $3 worth more of goods, on credit.

Uses ($)		Sources ($)	
Cash	2	The owner	10
Bank account	2	Owed to supplier	3
Stocks	9	Profits	1
Owed to business	1		
Total	14	Total	14

Three dollars more has come into the business, in the form of credit from a supplier, which is the same as a loan to the business.

11. The business sells goods which cost $5 for $7. The customer pays $3 in cash and is allowed credit for the balance of $4.

Uses ($)		Sources ($)	
Cash	5	The owner	10
Bank account	2	Owed to supplier	3
Stocks	4	Profits	3
Owed to business	5		
Total	16	Total	16

Ensure that every participant, and not just the one who suggests each transaction, fully understands the figures at each stage. More complex transactions should be gone through in detail, showing how each aspect of the transaction is reflected in the figures.

12. The customer who owed the earlier debt of $1 dies, and the debt has to be 'written off'.

Uses ($)		Sources ($)	
Cash	5	The owner	10
Bank account	2	Owed to supplier	3
Stocks	4	Profits	2
Owed to business	4		
Total	15	Total	15

13. A customer makes an advance deposit of $2 to reserve goods which she will take in the future.

Uses ($)		Sources ($)	
Cash	7	The owner	10
Bank account	2	Owed to supplier	3
Stocks	4	Profits	2
Owed to business	4	Customer deposit	2
Total	17	Total	17

The business owes the customer $2, until she takes the goods.

14. The customer who left the $2 deposit buys for $5 goods which cost the business $4, paying cash for the balance.

Uses ($)		Sources ($)	
Cash	10	The owner	10
Bank account	2	Owed to supplier	3
Stocks	nil	Profits	3
Owed to business	4	Customer deposit	nil
Total	16	Total	16

The business in total is 'worth' $1 less than before, but the owner's share of the total has gone up, because the sum owed by the business has gone down by $2 but the profit has gone up by $1.

15. The business borrows $5 from a money-lender, and spends this money on new stocks.

Uses ($)		Sources ($)	
Cash	10	The owner	10
Bank account	2	Owed to supplier	3
Stocks	5	Profits	3
Owed to business	4	Loan	5
Total	21	Total	21

16. The business pays the supplier his $3.

Uses ($)		Sources ($)	
Cash	7	The owner	10
Bank account	2	Owed to supplier	nil
Stocks	5	Profits	3
Owed to business	4	Loan	5
Total	18	Total	18

17. The business repays the money-lender's loan, plus $1 interest.

Uses ($)		Sources ($)	
Cash	1	The owner	10
Bank account	2	Owed to supplier	nil
Stocks	5	Profits	2
Owed to business	4	Loan	nil
Total	12	Total	12

The interest payment was an expense, just like wages or supplies.

18. The owner is tired of the business, so the remaining stock of goods which cost $5 are sold off at a loss, for $3, in cash.

Uses ($)		Sources ($)	
Cash	4	The owner	10
Bank account	2	Owed to supplier	nil
Stocks	nil	Loss/Profit	nil
Owed to business	4	Loan	nil
Total	10	Total	10

19. The owner decides to 'wind up' the business. She closes the bank account, gets the customer who owes $4 to pay his debt and takes her money back from the business into her own pocket.

Uses ($)		Sources ($)	
Cash	10	The owner	10
Bank account	nil	Owed to supplier	nil
Stocks	nil	Loss/Profit	nil
Owed to business	nil	Loan	nil
Total	10	Total	10

The business has now returned to the same position as it was in when it started.

20. Ask participants who have some accounting knowledge whether this approach is familiar to them; are balance sheets often used in this way?

They may comment that 'balance sheets' are not used like this; they are only prepared at the end of accounting periods, and are made up of the 'balances' of all the various accounts. The balance sheet is usually the last item to be prepared by an accountant, as a summary of all the other records.

They are right, but the purpose of this exercise has not been to show what traditional accountants do for the type of formal businesses which have traditional accounts (which their owners very often do not understand and rarely use except to satisfy legal requirements). The exercise should have shown all participants how easy it is to produce a simple financial 'still picture' of a business, at any time.

We shall now produce a 'moving picture', or statement of operations.

21. Write on the board a summary list of all the transactions:

a. The owner invests $10 in the business, in cash.
b. The business buys $6 worth of goods for cash, for resale.
c. The business sells for $4 in cash goods which cost $3.
d. The business puts $2 in a bank savings account.
e. The business sells goods which cost $2 for $3, on credit.
f. The business buys $5 worth of new stocks, for cash.
g. The credit customer pays $2 of her debt, in cash.
h. The owner takes $1 cash out of the business for her own use.
i. The business buys $3 worth more of goods, on credit.
j. The business sells $5 worth of goods for $7; the customer pays $3 in cash and is allowed credit for the balance of $4.
k. The customer who owed the earlier debt of $1 dies, and the debt has to be 'written off'.
l. A customer makes an advance deposit of $2 to reserve goods which she will take in the future.
m. The customer who left the $2 deposit buys for $5 goods which cost the business $4, paying cash for the balance.

46

n. The business borrows $5 from a money-lender, and spends this money on new stocks.
o. The business pays the supplier his $3.
p. The business repays the money-lender's loan, plus $1 interest.
q. The owner is tired of the business, so the remaining stock of goods which cost $5 are sold off at a loss, for $3, in cash.
r. The owner decides to 'wind up' the business; she closes the bank account, gets the customer who owes $4 to pay his debt and takes her money back from the business into her own pocket.

Ask participants to go through this list, and to select those transactions which belong in the statement of profit and loss. Allow up to ten minutes for this. Some participants will find difficulty in deciding which items are relevant.

Using the above list of transactions, the transactions to be included are: c, e, h, j, k, m, p and q. Only these involve the business in making a profit or a loss. Ask why items such as: a, b, d, f, g, i, l, n, o and r are not included.

Lead them to the conclusion that these transactions only involve money being moved from one form of use to another, such as when an amount owing to the business is changed to cash, because the bill is paid, or when new stocks are bought, moving money from 'cash' to 'stocks', or new money being brought into the business from the outside, such as from the owner, a bank or money-lender, a customer's deposit or supplier's credit. This is not money which has been earned by the business.

22. Ask participants to work out from the relevant transactions the result of the business during its life; is it the same as the result shown by the 'dynamic balance sheet' exercise?

Allow up to 15 minutes for this; elicit the following calculation:

	($)
Sales ($4+3+7+5+3)	22
Goods purchased ($6+5+3+5)	19
Margin	3
Expenses ($1+1+1)	3
Profit/loss	nil

23. It is difficult both to maintain the pace of this exercise and to ensure that all participants understand each stage of it. Remind participants that they should admit that they are confused if they are, and reassure them that the next session will give them an opportunity to reinforce what they have learned and to clarify points of uncertainty.

24. Ask any accountants in the group whether they prepare balance sheets and profit-and-loss accounts for businesses, or their NGOs, in this way. It is unlikely that any do. If time allows, ask an accountant very briefly to describe a standard double entry accounting system, using a cash book, day books, ledgers, trial balances and so on.

It should be clear that such systems are quite inappropriate for micro-enterprises, and that most NGO staff themselves cannot understand them. Show that the simple exercises in the last two sessions have demonstrated that it is actually quite easy to produce the two basic accounting statements, the balance-sheet and the profit-and-loss account, from a simple list of transactions.

Larger and more complicated enterprises need more complex accounting systems; accountants should be able to explain them to the people who will use them such as NGO staff, and NGO staff themselves should be able to make simple assessments of micro-enterprises and explain them to their owners, and to show them how to keep whatever simple records they may need. These records will be covered later in the course.

25. The enterprise experience businesses provide an ideal basis for applying what has been learned. Participants can make up 'still pictures' of their businesses, and change them after each transaction. They should approach their colleagues or the instructor if they are unsure about how a particular transaction should be entered.

The practical use of business figures

OBJECTIVE
To enable participants to make use of simple accounting figures in order to identify problems and recommend solutions to real businesses.

TIME
One and a half to two hours.

MATERIALS

Copies of 'Mary the shopkeeper', and 'Ali the carpenter' and of the handout 'Simple financial analysis for micro-enterprises', for all participants.

SESSION GUIDE

1. Remind participants that tomorrow they will have to apply what they are learning about accounts in the classroom to real businesses in the market. The figures will then not be clearly and unambiguously presented to them, but they will have to get them from the business people, identify and try to fill any gaps and then put the figures into the format of the 'still' and 'moving' pictures in order to be able to use them to advise the owner of the business.

This session will be 'half-way' towards that real-life situation; we shall be dealing with three case-studies, where figures will be provided in a realistic way, that is in no particular order, and perhaps with some gaps. Participants will have to put the figures in order, identify and try to fill any gaps and then analyse the completed statements and make suggestions as to possible improvements in financial management.

2. Distribute 'Mary the shopkeeper'. Allow up to ten minutes for participants to try to complete this on their own, and then encourage those who have not been able to finish to seek advice from their possibly more experienced neighbours; it is important that they should first try on their own.

After a further five minutes ask one participant to tell you what format to put on the board, into which you will then put the figures. Extract the necessary headings for the 'still' and the 'moving' pictures' of Mary's business, and put them on the board, without any figures.

Then go round the class asking each participant in turn to suggest where one figure should be written into the format you have prepared. Be sure not to allow one participant to give all the answers, since the objective is to make sure that even those with no previous knowledge of accounting are able to test and demonstrate their newly acquired skill.

49

3. The final figures should be as follows:

'Still' picture of Mary's shop on 31 December 1993

Uses ($)		Sources ($)	
Cash	50	Mary's money	200
Owed to business	200	Owed to supplier	100
Stocks	400	Loan	100
Bank savings	350		
Total	1000	Total	400

'Moving' picture of Mary's shop for December 1993

	($)
Sales	500
Cost of what was sold	400
Margin	100
Expenses: Mary's wage	50
Profit for month	50

4. Ask participants to suggest why the two columns of the 'still picture' do not balance; what figure is missing?

Help them reach the answer that if the other figures are correct, and there are no other missing items, the balance of $600 must have come from profits which Mary left in the business.

What other information is there which suggests that $1000 may indeed be the correct figure?

The profit for one month is $50, and the business has apparently been operating at a similar level for 12 months. It appears therefore that Mary has, without being aware of the fact, reinvested $50 a month in her business for 12 months, giving a total reinvestment of $600.

Point out that this is one way in which very simple accounts of this kind can be used to find out about the past history of a business. If the total value of what the business owns is well in excess of the sources that can be identified, this means that the owner has reinvested the profits. This is in fact the main source of money for most businesses once they have been going for some time.

Ask participants what other factor, apart from reinvested profits, can increase the value of what a business owns so that it far exceeds the identifiable sources. Inflation increases the value in money terms, and money is the only 'language' we have to compare values of different things. If a business bought a small building for $200 in 1980, for instance, it might be 'worth' $1000 in 1990, but this increase in value is in fact mainly caused by the reduction in the real value of money, not by an increase in the real value of the building. Inflation means that accounting figures are a less reliable way of assessing business results over a long period, and participants should be aware of this factor if the businesses they are assessing are more than a few years old.

5. Remind participants that the purpose of learning how to produce these figures is not to pass an exam. They are tools for understanding businesses and assisting yourself or others to manage them better, and if they are not used for this it is a waste of time to learn them.

The calculation of reinvested profits (or accumulated losses) is useful to assess the past performance of a business, and to help its owner recognize her success, or her failure. There are many other ways in which we can use even very simple figures such as we have now produced for Mary's business to assess the financial management and to make suggestions for improvement.

Ask participants what other comments they can make about the way in which Mary is managing the money in her business; does she appear to be allocating her money sensibly?

Some participants may be familiar with 'accounting ratios'; point out that every business is different, and there are no standard rules as to the correct relationships between amounts of money being used in different ways in a business. Ask participants to examine the figures in the 'Uses' column. What can they learn from them about Mary's financial management?

Participants may comment on the figures for stocks or for money owed to the business. Stress that the figures mean nothing unless they are related to other figures. What should these figures be related to?

Stocks ($400) should be related to the cost to the business of the goods sold each month (also $400); what does it mean that they are both the same? Mary's business has stocks for one month of sales. This might be too high for a shop selling perishable goods, and too low for a shop selling goods which are in short supply or where customers need to be able to see a wide range, but for a village general shop it is probably about right.

Money owed to the business ($200) should be related to the sales in a month ($500); what does this relationship mean?

Mary is giving credit for two-fifths of a month, or less than two weeks; as with all figures, this average may conceal a small number who owe for far longer periods, but the average seems reasonable.

Elicit comments on other relationships such as the following.

Money owed by the business ($100) to the cost of goods sold each month ($400); this means that Mary's business owes the cost of supplies for one-quarter of a month, or about one week.

Margin ($100) to sales ($500); this means that Mary is making a margin of one-fifth, or twenty per cent, on her sales. Or, for every dollar of sales, she earns twenty cents towards her costs.

Profit ($50) to sales ($500); this means that the business makes a ten per cent profit, or ten cents for every dollar of sales.

The savings ($350) *plus the cash* ($50) are together more than the total of the outstanding loan ($100), and the amount owed to the supplier ($100). This means that if Mary unexpectedly had to repay the loan, and her supplier, she would still be able to stay in business.

The cash and the savings, or what accountants call the 'liquid assets', that is, items under 'Uses' which could if necessary be used immediately to pay off the debts of the business, or its 'current liabilities', add up to $400. This is well over the total of $200 owed by the business to its supplier and to Mary's brother, so she could if necessary pay these debts and still stay in business.

Ask for comments on these 'ratios'. In general, they suggest that Mary is making good use of her money.

6. Distribute copies of 'Ali the carpenter'. Allow participants 15 minutes, at first on their own as before, to try to complete the assignment, and then encourage them to discuss it with one another.
   Elicit the figures as before, by asking each participant to deal with one item. The completed 'still' and 'moving' pictures should be as below.
   The details of sequence and layout are not important, if participants wish to have the 'sources' column on the left and the 'uses' column on the right, or if they prefer any particular sequence for the figures in each column, be guided by them. Do not try to impose the form; what matters is that they all understand the substance.

'Still' picture of Ali's carpentry business on 31 December 1993

Uses ($)		*Sources ($)*	
Cash	100	Ali's money	1000
Stocks – wood	500	Owed to supplier	500
Stocks – furniture	1000		
Owed by customers	1500		
Equipment	500		
Building	900		
Total	4500	Total	1500

'Moving' picture of Ali's carpentry business for December 1993

		$
Sales		500
Cost of wood and other materials		200
Margin		300
Expenses: Ali's wage	240	
Helper's wage	60	
Transport	30	
Tea etc.	20	
Total expenses		350
Loss for the month		50

7. Ask for comments and discussion. The following points should be covered:

- No allowance is made for 'depreciation' or the decline in value of the equipment. Explain that businesses such as taxis or large companies with very costly equipment which wears out or becomes out of date very quickly, should include some allowance for this in their expenses, to avoid overstating their profits, and to make sure that they are able to buy new equipment when it is needed. This is probably not necessary for very small businesses with very modest equipment, such as are typical of NGO clients, particularly because items such as carpenters' tools usually increase in value (because of inflation) faster than they decrease because they wear out.

- The business appears to have reinvested profits of $3000 ($4500 minus $1500) but inflation in the value of equipment and the shed has probably caused some of this. The business may have been making profits in the past, but it is losing money now.

- The business has stocks of raw materials for two and a half months ($500 stocks, $200 monthly cost). This is probably too much.

- The business has stocks of finished furniture for two months of sales ($1000 stocks, $500 sales). This is also probably too much.

- The customers owe the business three months of sales ($1500 owed, $500 sales). This is too long.

- Ali is paying himself a salary based on what he believes somebody with his skill should earn, rather than what the business can afford.

- The margin which Ali is adding over the cost of materials is one and a half times or 150 per cent of the cost of the materials themselves (margin $300 vs. materials $200). This may be normal, but it seems high for simple furniture making. If the margin is higher than Ali's competitors', this may mean that his prices are too high. High prices would explain the low sales and the resulting loss.

- The workload may not justify the employment of a helper. NGOs should not discourage employment, but it is even more important that businesses should not lose money. This is not in anybody's ultimate interest.

- Tea and snacks are pleasant but not essential. They should be paid for from personal earnings and not from a business – particularly a business which is losing money.

Some participants who are still more orientated towards larger formal businesses may say that items such as income taxes have been omitted. If they do, use this to re-emphasize the point that this course, and most NGO enterprise development, is directed at *really* small enterprises, which are usually far beneath the attention of income-tax authorities.

8. Distribute the handout 'Simple financial analysis for micro-enterprises'. Participants should read this through and be sure they understand it. They may also find it useful for analysing the figures they are to obtain from their visits to enterprises the next day. The 'ratios' are not given in the form of formulas, since participants should not try to memorize them. The purpose is to understand them, and to identify situations where they may be useful.

These and other points show how much can be learned from a few easy figures. Stress that such figures do not in themselves suggest what a business owner should do, they merely suggest questions that should be asked. There may be special circumstances such as shortage of supplies, competition or other reasons which fully justify all the apparent management mistakes identified above. Tomorrow participants will have to tease out whatever figures they can, and then ask appropriate questions in order to give useful advice.

9. Some participants may want hand-outs to remind them of the correct figures. It is better to ensure that they have all worked out and written down the correct figures for themselves. People learn more from what they have done for themselves than from papers that have been prepared for them.

DAY TWO — SESSION FOUR

Mary the shopkeeper

Mary started her small general shop, in the front of her own house, on 1 January 1993. It is now 31 December 1993 and Mary wants to know how well she has been doing. She has not kept any records, since she cannot read or write, but she has a very good memory. She says she felt that the business started well, and it has been going on at more or less the same level for the whole year.

You have interviewed her, and have obtained the following information from her:

She has $400 worth of stocks in the shop.
She pays herself $50 a month, every month.
She borrowed $100 from her brother, without interest, and has not repaid any of this amount.
She has $50 in the cash box belonging to the business.
She spends $400 a month on goods to be sold.
She put her own savings of $200 into the business when she started.
Her customers owe her $200 for goods bought on credit.
She sells $500 worth of goods every month.
Her passbook shows that she has accumulated savings of $350 since the business started.
She owes $100 to suppliers for goods bought on credit.

ASSIGNMENT

Prepare a 'still' and a 'moving' picture of Mary's business, showing the financial situation on 31 December 1993 and the financial operation of the business for a month.

What comments have you about Mary's management of her business?

DAY TWO — SESSION FOUR

Ali the carpenter

Ali started his carpentry business about ten years ago. He built a small shed, and started to make simple furniture for the local community, as he had learned when he had a job with another carpenter some years before. He keeps no records, but he has a reasonable memory for figures, and you have obtained the following information from him on 31 December 1993.

The shed is now worth $900.
He pays himself $240 a month from the business, since he says $8 is a proper
    daily wage for a carpenter.
He has $100 cash in the business.
The business owes $500 to its suppliers.
The monthly sales are $500.
The raw materials in stock are worth $500.
The monthly cost of wood and other materials is $200.
The completed products in stock are worth $1,000.
He has a helper who is paid $60 a month.
His customers owe the business $1,500.
He spends $20 a month from the business on tea and snacks for himself, the helper
    and his customers.
His tools and equipment are worth $500.
The business pays $30 a month for transport of materials.
He put his savings of $1,000 into the business when it started.

ASSIGNMENT

Prepare a 'still' and a 'moving' picture for Ali's business, showing the financial situation on 31 December 1993 and a 'moving picture' of the financial operation of the business for a month.
    What comments have you on Ali's management of his business?

DAY TWO — SESSION FOUR

Simple financial analysis for micro-enterprises

A balance sheet is a financial picture of a business, at a particular date. It is made up of the sources and the uses of money.

The sources of money for a business, or the liabilities, include the following items:

- The owner's capital invested in the business.

- Any outstanding loans.

- Any money owed by the business to others, such as suppliers.

- Advance deposits made by customers for goods not yet delivered.

- Profits reinvested in the business. (NB: This often has to be calculated, being the balancing figure between the total of the uses and of the sources. If it is a negative figure, this means accumulated losses.)

The uses of money in a business, or assets, include the following:

- Cash in hand, and bank balances.

- Money owed to the business by customers who have bought on credit.

- Stocks of materials, work in progress or finished goods.

- Tools, equipment and buildings.

The profit-and-loss account shows how the business has proceeded during a period, which may be a years, a month, a week or even a day. The profit (or loss) is the total sales made by the business for the period, less the total costs, including materials, labour, transport, administrative costs, allowance for wear and tear of equipment, interest on loans and all other costs.

You can use these figures to assess how well the owner of the business is managing the money invested in it. Here are some examples:

- The amount owed by customers divided by the sales per day gives the average period of credit allowed to customers.

- The amount of material stocks divided by the cost of materials per day gives the number of days' worth of material held in stock.

- The amount of finished goods stocks divided by the sales per day gives the number of days' worth of finished goods held in stock.

- The total of cash in hand divided by the sales per day gives the number of days' worth of cash held in the business.

- The total of the owner's capital and the reinvested profits divided by the total amount of money in the business shows the share of the total value of the business which is contributed by the owner.

- The annual profit, after allowing for the owner's salary, divided by the total of the owner's capital and reinvested profits, gives the annual profit as a percentage of the investment. This can be compared with other ways of using the money, such as putting it on deposit in a bank.

- The total of cash and bank balance can be compared with the total sum owed by the business which may be recalled without notice. This shows how secure the business is against a sudden withdrawal of credit.

- The total owed to suppliers by the business divided by the purchases per day shows the number of days' credit the business is getting.

- The total amount of reinvested profit divided by the number of years the business has been in existence shows the average amount of profit that the owner has left in the business each year.

NOTES All these items relate to only averages. It is perfectly possible for a short average period of credit to conceal a small number of very slow-paying accounts, or a short average period of stockholding to conceal a few seriously overstocked items.

These simple calculations, or 'ratios', cannot be judged without knowing something about the particular business. A fish-seller holds lower stocks than a jeweller, for instance, and businesses which sell to other businesses usually give far longer credit than businesses which sell directly to the public. The calculations do, however, show you what questions you ought to ask, and they provide the basis for any assessment of the quality of management.

How to obtain business information in the field

OBJECTIVE

To enable participants to collect information from the owners of micro-enterprises, and to use this as a basis for useful analysis and recommendations.

TIME

One hour.

NOTE Participants will spend most of this day in small groups in a nearby market, obtaining information and learning from local business people. If at all possible, the market should be within easy walking distance of the training place. If it is necessary to take a bus or car to a local market this may mean that the training institution is inappropriately sited for NGO staff training courses, which should always be as close as possible to the environment where their clients live and work.

The businesses should not be selected or warned before the interviews, since selecting a business and obtaining its owner's co-operation is an important lesson in itself. If local regulations require that the police or market committee are informed in advance, this must of course be done, but this is not usually necessary and every effort should be made to keep the whole exercise as informal and 'low key' as possible.

If possible, the market should not be well-known to the participants, and it is better if it is a completely unfamiliar place. In any case, the micro-enterprises whose owners are interviewed must not be receiving or be likely to receive any form of assistance from participants' organizations.

This session should be as brief as possible, so that participants can spend the maximum time in the market. Experienced field-workers may already be familiar with much of what follows, although probably not as applied to micro-enterprises. As with all these sessions, the material should be modified to suit the level of the participants.

It is usually better to have an introductory session of this sort at the beginning of the day when the field-work will actually be carried out, in order to ensure that the practical details are fresh in participants' minds and that all the groups start at the same time.

SESSION GUIDE

The objective of this session is to prepare participants for their subsequent meetings with business owners. They should take careful note of the various practical guide-lines for successful field interviews, which have been evolved as the result of many similar field-work exercises in the past.

Some participants may fear that they will be unable to persuade business owners to co-operate, to communicate effectively with them or to obtain the necessary information. Reassure them that it is not easy, but that many other people have successfully done what they are about to do, and that they will almost certainly be surprised by how willing the business owners are to help. They must take the right attitude at the beginning; this session is designed to help them do this.

The guide-lines will be dealt with in the sequence of the day's work:

- Preparation before going to the market.

- Selection of the business.

- Introducing yourselves to the business.

- Behaviour during the meeting.

- Obtaining information.

- Making recommendations.

2. PREPARATION

Divide participants into groups of up to three members. If necessary, participants can work on their own in this exercise, and groups of four or more should be avoided, since a large group may intimidate some business people, and some participants, particularly those who need to learn the most, may be tempted to let others do all the work.

Some more senior staff who are familiar with accounting may feel that this session is too elementary for them. They should be encouraged to help those who are less experienced, and such people are often quite remote from the reality of micro-enterprises; they may need this field exposure more than field staff.

Each group should include members with a balance of experience. Every effort should be made to interview one or more women business owners, and if the society is such that it is not easy for men to interview women, one or more groups should be made up of women alone. Ensure that each group has at least one member who can speak the local language. Ask the members of each group to sit together for the rest of this session.

After this session, and before leaving the classroom, each group should take a few minutes in order to:

- Allocate responsibilities for the various tasks.

- Draw up simple check-lists to avoid forgetting to ask any questions.

- Draw up a layout into which to insert the figures.

Do not provide any pre-prepared check-lists or guide-lines. Effective learning comes from what people do for themselves.

3. SELECTION OF THE BUSINESS

Try to avoid every group having the same sort of business. If appropriate, for instance, ask one group to select a retail business, another a service business, another a manufacturing or processing business and another a business owned by a woman.

Participants may feel that they must find a 'proper' formal business. Stress that they should work with really small 'informal' businesses, such as vegetable vendors, roadside mechanics or shoemakers, since these are the types of business which poor people engage in.

The businesses should not be too close to one another, since otherwise members of one group may drift to another, or the whole exercise may become a public meeting.

The businesses should not be ones with which any of the participants have had any previous contact, either as customers or, more importantly, as NGO clients.

Groups should select their own businesses, the businesses should not be fore-warned, since obtaining their co-operation is an important part of the exercise and they should not prepare themselves specially; the aim is to find out about the businesses as they really are.

The groups should not only interview the more obvious businesses, which are along the main road. The smallest businesses, and particularly those operated by women, are often 'invisible', and it may be necessary for the groups to ask members of the community to show them where such businesses are to be found.

It is important to be sure that the person interviewed is the owner of the business. Groups should check at once if they are speaking to the owner, and if he is not available they should excuse themselves and find another business.

The businesses should be as typical and ordinary as possible. Groups should not try to find the best looking, or the poorest looking, but just a typical informal micro-enterprise.

If the meeting with the first business goes exceptionally well, or if on the contrary unexpected problems are encountered at some point, groups may choose to meet a second business. They may then choose which set of information to present, or to present both if they wish.

Women's businesses are often harder to find, because in some places women have to work at home. It is worth making a special effort to find such businesses, because women's enterprises are usually the most needy, the most numerous and the most productive.

4. INTRODUCTIONS

The selected group leader should briefly introduce herself and the other participants by name to the business owner, and explain that the group would like, as a part of their training, to spend some time with him in order to learn from what he is doing.

It should be made clear that the group has come to *learn* from the business owner, and possibly to offer some tentative advice. They have not come to teach him, and, most important, they have *not* come in order to appraise or select candidates for loans. This point must be particularly stressed, since serious misunderstandings can arise if this is not made clear.

The group may express some admiration for the business and its products, and perhaps buy a product or service, such as a cup of tea from a tea-shop, a haircut from a barber or a shoe polish or small repair from a shoeshiner or cobbler.

5. BEHAVIOUR DURING THE MEETING

The discussion may easily take one or two hours or more, and it is important for all members of the group to demonstrate not only by what they say, but by what they do, that they really do respect the business owner and sincerely want to learn from him.

Only one member of the group should ask questions at one time. The others can take notes (see below), observe and wait until their allocated topic comes up.

All members of the group should work at the level of the business owner. If this means squatting on a dusty roadside or standing by a hot furnace, so be it.

The business owner may suspect that the group is in some way connected with the authorities, who usually harass informal businesses. Members of the group must make it clear that they are not, by saying so, and by their behaviour.

It is better not to stand over the business owner with a clipboard or large pad or exercise book. Use a very small notebook, and be at the same or a lower level than the business owner, so that he dominates you, not the reverse.

The business owner is being asked to share confidential personal information with the group, and may not want his customers and competitors to hear it all. Try if possible to hold the discussion in a semi-private place, such as in the back of the stall, rather than in the open street or market-place. This is particularly important for women's businesses.

It may be difficult to communicate directly with women business owners, since men from the community will try to answer for them. Participants should try to avoid this. Some members of a group may take the men away under the pretext of asking for more information, or the women in the group may go with the women into their private quarters.

Unlike NGO staff, owners of informal businesses lose personally if they do not work productively at all times. The group should avoid making the business lose any customers, and should stand aside even if the owner prefers to ignore his clients. This is in itself a useful piece of advice by example.

6. INFORMATION GATHERING

The previous sessions have concentrated on financial information, because this is the basis of business analysis, and NGO staff are usually less confident in the area of finance than in other areas. The groups should not concentrate only on the financial data, however; one reason for spending time in the business itself is that this is the only way to find out about the quality of the products and the way the owner markets his goods or services.

The earlier exercises have provided participants with all the financial information, 'on a plate'. There are a few simple techniques which make it easier to get this and other non-financial information from business owners in the field.

The owner's answers are only one source of information. We can observe things like the quantity and condition of goods in stock, the quality of products, the way the owner treats customers and the appearance of the business to an outsider. All four senses can be used. The sense of touch can detect old stock by feeling dust, and even the sense of smell can detect rotten or damp items in storage.

One member of the group should be assigned the task of making the necessary calculations as quickly and accurately as possible, in order to identify major inconsistencies and to work towards any recommendations which may appear to be appropriate.

The owner may not give correct information, because he does not know it, he does not understand our questions or he does not wish to give it. Information can be obtained in many different ways. Ask participants, for instance, to suggest ways of finding out the daily sales of a tea-shop ask questions like the following:

- What is the daily sales figure in money?

- How many cups of tea are sold each day?

- How many kilos of sugar or of tea are used each day, and how many cups of tea can be obtained from one kilo?

Few informal businesses keep any written records, if only because their owners are often illiterate. The owner may be proud to show his books if he does have any, and they can provide some information, but they can often be out of date, wrong or irrelevant.

7. RECOMMENDATIONS

Groups should try to give some advice to the businesses they meet, both as a small recompense for the time spent by the owner in talking to them and in order to develop their skill in using business information to improve management, instead of just obtaining it.

It is obviously important to avoid giving wrong information which may, if the owner follows it, actually damage or even destroy the business. Most business owners are shrewd enough not to be misled by inexperienced outsiders, however well-qualified they may appear to be, but there are some guide-lines which groups should follow.

Group members should follow the method adopted in this training course, by attempting whenever possible to 'elicit' recommendations from the business owner himself, rather than merely telling him what he should do. Business owners, like the course participants, are far more likely to accept and follow suggestions if they feel they 'own' them, because have themselves suggested them.

One way of recommending a vendor to draw up a simple poster to advertise a special price is to tell him what to do. Ask participants to suggest another way which might be more successful.

They might ask the business owner how passing customers are expected to know about the special price, if they do not ask and if they do not hear him shouting about it. He might not have any ideas. They might then ask him to walk out into the street and to look at the larger shops; what does he see which he might copy? He should then realize that he too might advertise his special price with a sign as well as by shouting about it; the idea will then be his, which will increase his chance of implementing it.

Basic recommendations such as cleaning the floor or putting up a poster may be just as appropriate as financial management suggestions such as limiting or recording credit sales, disposing of slow-moving stocks or reducing the owner's own wages.

Groups should explain their analysis to the business owner and ask him what he thinks of it. They should terminate the meeting by thanking him and asking his advice as to what NGOs such as their own can do to help business people in general. Again, they should not give the impression that they are offering to help him individually.

8. ASSIGNMENT

Each group will have to present on the following day their results of the following assignment.

a. Briefly describe the business, its history and the person who owns it. Why did (s)he start it, and how?

b. Prepare a simple 'still' picture of the financial position of the business, today, and a 'moving' picture showing its performance over a typical recent period, which may be a day, a week, a month or a year, depending on what is most appropriate.

c. Briefly describe the business owner's opinion as to what are his main problems, and the group's own view, if this is different.

d. Describe and explain whatever recommendations the group made to the owner, and his response.

e. What does the group recommend that NGOs should do, if anything, to assist business people of this kind?

Stress that it may take two hours or more to complete this assignment properly, even with an apparently very simple business. If time allows, however, the groups may interview two businesses; this is particularly interesting in a community where a whole industry is based, and where different businesses trade with one another in order to produce a complete product.

9. NEXT SESSION

Participants must complete their meetings with business owners in time to return to the classroom for the next session. If they finish earlier, they can visit another business, and they can of course start their analysis before the next session, but they will be surprised how long it takes to obtain all the necessary information from a business, and properly to 'get a feel' for the way it operates. The meetings must not be rushed.

Remind the participants to spend a few minutes organizing their group for the field visits, and wish them success.

The micro-enterprise interviews, and subsequent presentations, are fundamental to the whole course, and they must not be omitted under any circumstances. Some participants may be reluctant to go into the market if it is raining, or very hot, or if it is a public holiday or festival they may say that the businesses will be closed. Stress that micro-enterprises have to operate in the rain, and often on days when 'official' organizations are closed, because their owners do not receive regular salaries; they earn nothing when they are not working. Participants must be willing to do the same if they are to understand and effectively assist them.

Group meetings with business owners

OBJECTIVE

To enable participants to meet and learn from the owners of micro-enterprises, to collect information, analyse it and make appropriate recommendations.

TIME

Three hours or more.

This period for gathering information is of course not a classroom session; participants will be working on their own and the instructor's role is limited.

It is important that the groups should be told to re-assemble in the classroom at a specific time for the next session, since this will ensure that they remain in the market for enough time. It will also discourage them from staying in the market too long rather than returning to complete their analysis and to prepare their presentation for the next day.

The instructor should also go to the area where the groups are meeting business owners, but should not accompany or help them, since one purpose of this exercise is to enable participants to work on their own with their clients.

You should if possible try to observe each group 'in action', without playing any part in the meeting. You should note one or two points about the business, to remind you which one it is when the group make their presentation the next day. You may also be able to notice some important aspect such as the lack of any signboard or the way in which the stocks are kept which you can mention during the presentations if the group has missed them.

You should also observe the way the group is interacting with the business owner. If they are making any obvious serious errors you may have to intervene in order to 'rescue' the situation, but you should otherwise merely note down any aspects of their behaviour which may be worth discussing the next day.

It is possible that one or more groups may complete their assignment too quickly; it is most unlikely that the necessary information can be obtained in less than an hour, and it is more likely to take two hours. If you find a group which appears to be going away too soon, ensure that they have got all the information they need. If they have not, they should return to the business, and if they have they should identify another business as was suggested in the previous session.

Presentation skills

OBJECTIVE

To enable participants to present business information correctly, clearly and concisely.

TIME

Half an hour.

MATERIALS

Groups will need newsprint or flip-chart sheets and the necessary pens, or some other presentation media. It is better not to use overhead transparency sheets, since the completed financial data should be displayed in the classroom for the rest of the course. Each group may need to present up to six or seven sheets, and some allowance should also be made for spoiled sheets.

NOTE The main purpose of this session is to ensure that participants prepare their presentations properly, and it is therefore scheduled after the field visits. If the presentations themselves are scheduled to take place immediately following the meetings with business owners, there is a danger that participants will spend too much time in the field, or that they will not take the analysis and preparation tasks seriously enough. This session should take place late enough to allow time for the meetings with business owners but early enough to allow participants time to analyse the information they have obtained and to prepare a convincing and 'slick' presentation.

Participants will need to be told during this session how much time they will have for their presentations. The whole of the morning of Day Four has been allowed for this. The time for each group will depend on the number of groups, but you should allow at least five minutes after each presentation for questions and discussion, and at least 30 minutes at the end for general conclusions.

SESSION GUIDE

1. Remind participants that presentation skills are an important part of the work of NGO staff. Ask them if they have any experience of presenting information to groups of people, and mention important groups to whom it is often necessary to present information, such as:

- Organizations which provide funds for the NGO.

- Members of the communities where the NGO is starting work.

- Colleagues, for instance, after this course, in order to share whatever was learned.

They should use the forthcoming presentations as an opportunity to practise and improve their presentation skills, as well as sharing the business information they have obtained.

2. Each group will have a maximum of 15 minutes to make its presentation, followed by 10 minutes of questions and discussion. They need not of course use all this time. (These times should be modified according to the number of groups.)

Groups may organize their presentations in any way they choose, but they should ensure that their presentations cover the five separate topics of:

- Description of the business and its owner.

- The 'still' and the 'moving' financial pictures.

- The problems of the business, as perceived by its owner and the group.

- The recommendations the group made, and the owner's reactions.

- The group's conclusions as to the role of NGOs.

Groups should be encouraged to allocate different sections of their presentations to different members, to give as many participants as possible the chance to practise their presentation skills.

3. Remind participants of the brief introduction to presentation skills in Session Four of the first day, and of the presentations which they made about their enterprise experience plans on the second day. Recall any lessons they learned at that time about how to make convincing presentations.

Groups will have to communicate a great deal of information in a short period. They will need to be selective and clear, since it is better to succeed in putting across a small amount of data than to fail in putting across a large amount.

Stress the following points:

- The sequence must be clear.

- Visual aids should contain only a few key words and figures, not whole sentences or long complicated figures. It is probably better to put the 'still' and the 'moving' pictures on different sheets.

- Figures should when necessary be 'rounded'. They are unlikely to be completely accurate in any case, and it is not necessary that they should be – this is not an audit.

- Calculations must be correct, without exception.

- Groups should not present or discuss general views about micro-enterprises or the difficulty of obtaining financial information about them. Presentations must focus on the individual enterprises and in particular on the analysis of financial data obtained from them, however sketchy and confused it may appear.

- The timing will be strictly enforced, groups should perhaps practise their presentations to ensure that they are not too long.

4. Participants should now prepare their analysis and prepare their presentations.

Business presentations

OBJECTIVE
To enable participants to present and share the information they have obtained and the conclusions they have reached, in order to develop a view of the needs and problems of informal businesses which is based on reality.

TIME
Three to four hours.

SESSION GUIDE

1. As with the enterprise experience presentations on Day Two, do not reveal the sequence in which groups will make their presentations. As before, nominate two participants as 'commentators' for each group. One must comment on the presentation style, and another on the content. Invite the first group to make its presentation. If they wish, they can accept and deal with questions as they are speaking, but they must still keep within the time limit. The group may prefer other participants who wish to comment or ask questions to wait until the group has finished.

2. Maintain the time limit strictly. Warn the group when they have two minutes left, and do not allow any extra time.

3. When the first group has finished, ask the 'style' commentator briefly to make any comments. She should refer to items such as:

- The clarity and legibility of any visual aids.

- The way in which the speakers presented their material. Did they speak clearly? Did they face and look at the audience or at the floor? Did they appear to understand the content of what they were presenting?

The instructor should only add points which have been omitted by the nominated commentator. People rarely have an opportunity to receive frank feedback about the presentation skills. Do not allow yourself or other participants to be too 'kind' from a misplaced sense of courtesy.

4. Ask the content commentator to make any comments. These should concentrate on points such as:

- The calculations, were they correct and clear? (Participants should realize that the mathematics involved are only arithmetic, maybe of class three or four standard. Any mistakes are the result of carelessness and not ignorance!)

- Were the figures suspiciously neat and 'balanced'. Did the group make unwarranted assumptions, rather than probing more deeply into the reasons for apparent inconsistencies in the figures?

- Were any important items missed?

- Was the analysis correct, and do the conclusions and recommendations follow logically from it?

- Were the group's conclusions as to the role of NGOs appropriate to what they actually discovered in the field?

5. Proceed as above with the remaining groups.

6. After every group has finished, promote a general discussion by posing questions such as the following. These raise issues which will be dealt with in more detail later in the course, and each could occupy many hours of discussion. It is useful to raise them now, in the context of the businesses which participants have visited.

- Why did the business owners start their businesses, and how did they obtain the skills and finance which were necessary? Would the kinds of assistance which NGOs provide have been of any help?

- If the businesses were keeping written records, were they making effective use of them? If they had no records, would written records have been of any real value to them, assuming that they knew how to keep them?

- Were the businesses suffering from harassment from the police or other authorities? Is such harassment justified in the public interest, or only in the interest of the minority or of the officials who may take bribes in return for not harassing informal businesses? What can or should an NGO do about such harassment?

- Had any of the businesses ever received loans from banks or other 'official' sources. If they had not, why not, and what could NGOs do to improve the situation?

- Did the businesses have difficulty in marketing their goods and services? If so, how might they be helped to sell more, and how, if at all, could NGOs help them?

- Were some of the 'businesses' actually just wage workers employed on a piece-work basis in their homes? If so, is it wise for NGOs to try to organize them or otherwise make them into independent businesses? Should they not be treated like any other employees?

- Did some of the businesses appear to be 'exploited' by 'middlemen'? Were the middlemen performing an essential linkage function, and could an NGO or other organization perform the same or better function and allow the business people to earn more money?

- Did some groups suggest that NGOs should 'organize', train or otherwise intervene, when the business owners were actually earning a reasonable wage? The best thing for an NGO to do may be to leave people alone!

If time allows, compare participants' conclusions with their attitudes as expressed during the Second Session of Day One.

7. Some participants may have allowed their enterprise experience businesses to lie dormant during the period of the field visits and presentations, because there was not enough time. Ask participants to identify critical differences between their own motivation in the enterprise experience and the business owners they met in the market.

Lead them to the answer that participants do not depend on their enterprise experience businesses in any but a very superficial way. If they lose money, the amounts will be small in relation to their incomes, and they can pick up or neglect the business as they wish.

Real informal business owners depend critically on their businesses for their own and their families' very survival. There is no sick pay or pension fund, and their income can suffer even from a few minutes' neglect of the business.

8. Finally, remind participants of the people and businesses which they have learned so much about. These business owners should form an unseen 'jury' for the rest of the course. The financial data should be displayed on the walls for the rest of the course, and participants should test what they are learning by reference to them.

What are NGOs, and what is their role in enterprise development?

OBJECTIVE   *To enable participants to describe the strengths and weaknesses of NGOs and their staff, and thus to identify the implications for their work in enterprise development.*

TIME   *One to one and a half hours.*

SESSION GUIDE

1. Point out that NGOs are a relatively new phenomenon, at least in the variety of work they now do, and that their nature and role are less clear than that of the more familiar public and private sectors. They are also being asked to carry out large numbers of tasks which are quite different from those which they traditionally carried out, and they now often act as contractors, to local or foreign donors. They are paid to implement 'projects', as well as, or perhaps instead of, pursuing the social goals for which they may originally have been established.

It is therefore very important to examine their nature, their origins and their funding sources, in order to be clear as to what they can and cannot do.

2. Acronyms or sets of initials often lead us to use terms without being clear as to their meaning. Ask a participant to say what the words 'non-governmental organization' mean in themselves.

The words themselves state only what they are *not*: NGOs are not part of government. Neither are private profit-seeking companies, and we are probably agreed that these are not what we mean by NGOs. The term in itself therefore tells us very little about what NGOs actually *are*.

3. Ask participants to suggest other words or acronyms which are used to describe the same sort of organizations. Encourage terms such as 'charities', 'voluntary societies' or 'PVOs' ('private voluntary organizations', which is the term used mainly in the USA). What do these terms tell us about the type of organizations they describe?

Ask participants what the word 'voluntary' means. It usually refers to people who are volunteers, that is, they work without any payment. How many of the participants do not receive any salaries for their work with an NGO? There may be some true 'volunteers', but most full-time workers at any rate need to be paid. Participants may or may not be earning salaries which are significantly lower than they could earn elsewhere, but most NGO staff work for reasonable salaries and are in no sense volunteers. It is a job like any other.

Ask a participant what the words 'charity' and 'social' mean. These words relate to the religious or social obligation that better-off people should give money to the poor out of sympathy for them.

Remind participants of their responses to the attitude questionnaire at the beginning of the course. There is clearly some inconsistency between charging for services, and making loans at market rates of interest which must be repaid, and the activities that are normally associated with 'charity' or 'social work'.

4. Ask participants to suggest what may have been the origins of their own and other NGOs. Who started them, and why?

Many NGOs were and still are started by religious people, who believe that they have an obligation to serve those who are less fortunate than themselves. Other NGOs have been begun by people who were working for government or for private businesses who become frustrated at the apparent failure of the private and the public sector to serve the best interests of humanity in general.

Some NGOs are set up in response to a particular crisis, such as a dam-construction project, where it seems that the economic interests of the minority are being allowed to prevail over the wider interests of the poorer and less-articulate majority. Still other NGOs are started in order to help a particular oppressed group – such as refugees or urban or rural migrant labourers – to come together to resist private business interests and to gain a fairer share of the economic 'cake' for themselves.

What are the implications of these different origins when these NGOs become involved in enterprise development?

5. Ask participants to identify the sources of funding for their NGOs. Who sponsors their work, and why?

Some of these sources are wealthy private individuals who establish NGOs and provide core funding. Many NGOs also rely to a considerable extent on voluntary contributions from the general public. The motives of these donors are usually the same as those of people who work as volunteers: they feel they have an obligation to help those less fortunate than themselves.

Foreign governments and NGOs support the work of many NGOs, for a very complex mix of reasons, which may include political, economic and social motives.

Government departments and public sector banks and other organizations sponsor individual projects. This is often because they recognize that NGOs are more competent at organizing such activities than they are themselves.

Large private companies sponsor many NGOs, for a variety of reasons. They may wish to improve their public 'image'; they may feel guilty about the impact of their activities on local people; or their management may have a genuine social concern, which they prefer to exercise with their company's money rather than their own.

Again, what are the implications of these funding sources for work in enterprise development?

6. Ask participants to write down a one-sentence summary of the views that all these terms, origins, motives and funding sources would suggest NGO staff might have on each of the following issues:

• The impact of business on society.

• The relative importance of economic growth vs equitable distribution.

• The necessity for their work to be self-sustaining.

Allow ten minutes for this, and then ask a participant to read out what she has written for the first issue. Opinions will of course differ, but the following view is consistent with the origins of most NGOs:

'Business, particularly but not only big business, is bad for society.'

Do the same for the other two issues, and elicit sentences such as:

'Equity is more important than growth.'

'Our work must always depend on donations.'

Clearly there are inconsistencies between these views and the development of business enterprise. This in part explains why NGOs have only in recent years started to become involved in enterprise development.

7. It is probable that most of the participants hold some of these views. Their views may or may not limit the effectiveness in the field of enterprise development, but they should at least be aware of the implications.

It may be useful to challenge some or all of the above statements by asking counter questions such as:

- If you believe that business is bad for society, why are you promoting business? If you only disapprove of big business, are you unconsciously denying your clients the opportunity to grow?

- It is often the case that one or two relatively richer entrepreneurs can create far more sustainable jobs for other people than those people could create for themselves. Is it better for everyone to be very poor or for most people to be less poor and a few people to be much richer?

- If NGOs always have to depend on donations, how can they ever reach more than a small proportion of the people who need their services?

8. Participants themselves may or may not hold these views; the attitude questionnaire at the beginning of the course will have enabled them to recognize and articulate their own opinions. Even if they do not hold these views themselves, however, other people certainly do. Ask who these may be, and how their views will affect participants in their own work.

Colleagues in the same NGOs, particularly those working in more 'traditional' NGO fields such as health, community development or education, may strongly oppose policies which contradict their views.

Donors may object to their funds being used in what appear to them to be 'commercial' ways. They may be enthusiastic about the idea of enterprise development, but dislike the practical implications.

The clients of an NGO may themselves may hold these views about NGOs. They will therefore find it difficult to accept that they may have to pay fees for services, or to repay loans, with interest.

9. One objective of this session is to help participants develop arguments to persuade such people to change their views; it is important to respect such opinions, whether or not we agree with them, and to be aware of their origins and their implications.

Some participants may come from NGOs which are new to enterprise development work, or they may have come on the course because their NGO plans to start working in this field.

They must appreciate the different attitudes which some of their colleagues may have, and the different 'image' which some members of the communities where they work may have of the NGO. They should not underestimate the difficulty, and the importance, of confronting these views and changing them.

Women and micro-enterprise

OBJECTIVE   *To enable participants to identify the particular problems and opportunities which face women in micro-enterprises.*

TIME   *One to one and a half hours.*

NOTE The guide for this session is written on the assumption that there are at least some women participants on the course, and that there are also some men. If there are no women at all, or if there are only women, you will have to make some changes.

SESSION GUIDE

1. Ask participants who are the most numerous owners and workers in micro-enterprises in their areas: women or men? Their answers will of course differ according to local circumstances, but in most places women play the most important part. Stress again that we are concerned with the very smallest enterprises. Participants may even now tend to think of the more visible formal businesses, where men certainly predominate, rather than the smallest economic activities of the poor.

Compare the importance of men and women in micro-enterprises to the relative proportions of men and women on the course. If (as is all too common) men make up the vast majority of participants, ask whether this matters. Stress that the proportions of men and women employees in NGOs, and still more in larger firms, banks and government reflect the imbalances in society at large. This session is designed to examine the situation in the context of micro-enterprises, and to help participants identify ways in which they themselves can make a difference.

2. Ask each married male participant to say whether his wife earns an income, either through employment or self-employment. Ask those whose wives do not earn an income to say why. If there are no married men, or all their wives earn an income, ask why so many women do not.

Look for reasons such as:

• Too much work at home.

• The children need their mother's care.

• Husband's income is enough

3. Ask each participant to think of a poor woman with a family whom he knows well, or if they do not know a poor woman to think of their own wives or mothers. They should write down a typical day's schedule for the woman they have thought

of, starting with the moment she gets up until the time she goes to sleep at night. Allow five minutes for this and then ask them to think of a poor man and allow the same time for them to write a similar schedule for his day.

Ask a woman participant to read out what she has written about a woman's day. Write a summary with times and tasks on one side of the board, and ask other participants to add items. Then do the same for a typical poor man's day on the other side of the board.

Ask participants to compare the two typical schedules. Relate them to their earlier explanations of why their wives do not earn an income, because of the household workload that is undertaken mainly by women.

4. Ask participants to put themselves in the position of the poor men and women whose daily lives have been described. If they need to earn more money, which are more likely to be able to find jobs, the poor men or the poor women?

Elicit the answer that although jobs are scarce for everyone, men are more likely to get some form of employment than women. Name some of the reasons for this, such as: men are more likely to have the necessary skills. Or, men can leave home and travel to find work.

Many poor women are the only or the main earners for their households. If they cannot find jobs with other people, what option remains for them? Elicit the answer that self-employment is often the only option, for reasons such as the following. First, micro-enterprises can often be run from home, and can thus be combined with domestic work. Second, micro-enterprises can be run on a part-time or seasonal basis, and so fit in with domestic and farm work. Finally, women lack the formal education necessary for getting jobs.

5. Women are therefore often forced to employ themselves, and to start micro-enterprises. Although women's enterprises are not always the most visible, and are certainly not the largest, they are usually the most numerous – even in communities where women are expected to remain at home.

6. Write the following brief assignment on the board:

You are a manager of an NGO and you have to decide which of two possible micro-enterprise support projects to start. Project A will enable 1000 of the poorest men in a community to add $10 a week to their incomes, and Project B will enable 1000 of the poorest women to do the same. Both projects will cost the same, and you can only choose one. Identify as many reasons as possible in favour of A and of B, and then decide which will you choose and why.

If time allows, divide participants into groups, each if possible including some women, and allow them up to twenty minutes to complete this. If there is not enough time for group work, allow participants ten minutes on their own to complete the assignment.

7. Ask each group or individual to state which of the two projects they will support. Divide the board into two sections, one for each project, and write the total numbers in favour of A and B above its respective half of the board. Participants may support Project B because the session relates to women, and they think they should. Be sure to list arguments in favour of both projects, and explain that participants must be

able to understand both points of view if they wish to be able to argue in favour of one of them.

Bring out the arguments in favour of each project, including the following:

Project A:

- Men are more likely to be able to get loans for later expansion.
- Men have better access to materials and to customers.
- Men are better educated and have more skills.
- Men are physically stronger.
- Men are free to travel as their business requires.
- Men are more likely to have had business or employment experience.
- Men dominate society; change will be difficult and disruptive.
- Men's enterprises are more likely to be able to expand in the future.
- Men are not diverted by childbirth and family care.

Project B:

- Women need self-employment more than men.
- Women save more regularly.
- Women repay loans more reliably.
- Women work harder and are more committed.
- Men are less likely to work hard for a small sum of money.
- Women spend their earnings on their families, not on liquor.
- Women need desperately to be 'empowered'.
- If group action is needed, women are better collaborators.
- Men can get jobs; women have no other options.
- Women need to be able to earn money at home.

8. Encourage discussion leading to the general conclusion that the decision must to an extent depend on the objectives of the NGO. If the intention is to help people establish enterprises with growth potential and to employ more people and earn more money, it may, although this is by no means certain, be better to support Project A.

Ask participants to suggest what are the objectives of their own NGOs. If an NGO wishes to work towards changes in society and to correct social injustice, it should probably support Project B.

9. Women's 'empowerment' differs from one country to another, and between different communities and income groups within each country, but generally speak-

ing women's economic, social and political position is worse in poorer countries than in rich ones.

Ask participants to guess the average life expectancy of women and of men in the poorer countries; the 1991 figures were:

	Men	Women
Poorer countries	61 years	58 years
Richer countries	73 years	80 years

If possible compare these and the following figures with figures for participants' own countries. Ensure that participants recognize not only that the average is higher in richer countries, but that women have shorter lives than men in poorer countries and live longer than men in rich countries.

Encourage discussion as to why this is the case, and elicit suggestions such as:

- Unequal access to health-care facilities

- High mortality rates in childbirth

- Harder working lives

10. Women usually share with their families whatever income they can earn, but they also have less opportunity to earn good incomes. Ask participants to guess the female proportion of the employed labour force in poorer and richer countries; the 1991 figures were:

	Men	Women
Poorer countries	66%	34%
Richer countries	56%	44%

11. One reason for this is women's lack of education. Ask participants to guess the percentage of adult men and women who are illiterate in the poorer and the richer countries; the 1991 figures were:

	Men	Women
Poorer countries	40%	48%
Richer countries	4%	5%

12. Participants should conclude that women everywhere, particularly in poorer countries, are seriously disadvantaged. They do a large part of the world's work, but, receive a very small part of the rewards of this work, in terms of money which they can control, wealth and social position.

This is not only unjust, but it is also uneconomic, since resources, such as food, capital and education, should be allowed to flow to the people who can make best use of them. Self-employment can help to correct this situation, and NGOs can help women to become successfully self-employed. There are therefore strong reasons for giving preference to women in enterprise development programmes.

13. The requirement in the earlier exercise to choose between Projects A and B was clearly unrealistic, since most projects deal with both men and women; nevertheless enterprise development workers, like anyone else in development, often have to chose between different options, some of which may benefit women more or than others.

Ask participants what they themselves can do in their work, in however modest a way, to correct the inequity of women's position. Ask for suggestions such as:

- allow and encourage women clients to speak for themselves
- arrange meetings at places and times which are convenient for women
- hire more women as field-workers and in senior positions
- facilitate women's access to finance and other resources.

Participants may feel that these policies will necessarily involve greater costs and lower success rates. Stress that women are generally better clients than men. Particularly if an NGO is involved in savings and credit, its programme is more likely to achieve self-sustainability if some parts of the transaction can be delegated to client groups, and if repayment rates are high. Women clients are more likely to be able to help a programme to do this than men.

Group or individual enterprise?

OBJECTIVE
To enable participants to analyse the advantages and disadvantages of group enterprises; and to identify situations where group, or individual enterprise may be appropriate.

TIME
One and a half to two hours.

MATERIALS AND ADVANCE PREPARATION

Copies of the case study, The Basket Makers' Society, or a modified version which is more relevant to the particular communities with which participants are working, should be given to all participants at the end of Day Four. They should be asked to work in the same groups into which they have already been organized for the field visits and to complete the assignment ready for this session.

SESSION GUIDE

1. Ask the spokesperson for one group to present their conclusions as to the mistakes which Simon made. List them on the board, using the group's own words when possible.

2. Ask each other group in turn to identify any other mistakes which they think the earlier groups have missed. The following notes summarize the major mistakes. Elicit any items which participants have omitted, by asking appropriate questions.

- The people themselves did not initiate the idea of the society, and nobody made any plan as a basis for deciding whether the society would be viable or not.

- Simon assumed that a co-operative would be able to do everything the middlemen did, and still pay the people more.

- Simon encouraged the weavers to have unrealistic expectations of what they might gain from the new society. The middlemen may indeed have been making extortionate profits, but they were also performing essential functions which cost money. The new society would have to perform these tasks instead of the middlemen, and their cost would have to be paid by the village people. They should not have been led to expect that they would get the whole of the final selling price of the baskets themselves.

- The ABC NGO provided grants to people who formed societies. This may have distorted their motives and encouraged them to form a society without really thinking through what was involved. Such special concessions are a form of 'bribe' which should not be needed if there is a genuine case for starting a society.

- Simon welcomed the village élite in the society; they may well have been working with the middlemen, and their interests would in any case not be the same as the basket makers'. They had perhaps 'hijacked' the society and tried to take it over to exploit the people and to run it for their own profit.

- Simon invited a local politician to be involved. He would most likely have been interested only in getting more voters for the elections. He might later have lost interest or even collaborated with the middlemen or the local élite to exploit the people.

- Simon encouraged the new society to attempt to carry out a number of complex business tasks. In addition to the middlemen's traditional functions of raw material supply and local sales, they became involved in design, credit and the development of new marketing outlets. This was too much.

- Simon did not take full responsibility for managing the society, but nor did he allow their own manager to manage it on his own. The responsibility was not clear.

- The ABC NGO more than once 'bailed out' the new society by making grants when it was in trouble. This may have led the members to believe that they would never have to take real responsibility for its success or failure.

3. Summarize the lessons that Simon should have learned from this experience, in the form of a simple list of guide-lines for NGO staff who may be involved in promoting group enterprises. Write them on the board, using participants' own words when possible. This might include the following:

- Avoid exaggerated expectations.

- Avoid 'bribes'.

- Avoid 'hijacking'.

- Avoid politicians.

- Avoid complexity – keep it simple.

- Avoid unclear responsibilities.

- Avoid 'bail-outs'.

4. There are obviously a great many dangers associated with group enterprises which are not so likely to affect individual businesses. Ask participants what they know about the success record of group enterprises, and official co-operatives in particular; it is generally bad, everywhere.

Ask participants what form of enterprise has been the driving force for the development of every national economy, everywhere. Clearly, co-operatives have played an important role in many countries, particularly in agriculture and credit, but individual private businesses have been the major 'engine of development'.

Refer to participants' enterprise experience businesses. They were free to set up individual enterprises, partnerships or larger group enterprises. There was nothing to prevent them from having established one group enterprise for all of them, with no risk of competition or duplication, why did they not do this?

5. Ask participants to suggest why they, and most other people who start businesses without any external advice or intervention, usually start individual or small partnership businesses; what are the weaknesses of group or co-operative enterprises? Encourage suggestions such as:

- Decision-making is slow.

- It is easy for some members to leave the work to others.

- Groups can be 'hijacked' by special interests.

- Groups are often permanently dependent on outside agencies.

- It is harder to manage a group business than an individual one, because the members have to be persuaded and informed while workers have only to do what they are told.

- People management is harder than in individual businesses.

6. Remind participants about their answers to the question in the attitude questionnaire about group enterprises. Many NGO staff, as well as people in government, believe that group enterprises are the best form of organization for poor people's businesses, in spite of their poor record. Ask participants to write down as many reasons as they can why they *should* promote group enterprises.
   Allow up to ten minutes for this, and draw out arguments like the following:

- The poor are weak and have few resources, but they are many. If they pool their resources, they can achieve economies of scale.

- The poor lack access to resources such as finance. They can gain their rights by working together.

- Women are usually the poorest people in poor communities. They are also the most effective group workers.

- If poor people set up individual businesses, they too will exploit their fellows. They may become rich only at their expense.

- Even if individual businesses tend to be more successful and to grow faster, they exaggerate society's inequalities. We should promote more equitable distribution through group enterprises.

- Poor communities often have strong traditions of community action. These can be used as a basis of new community business enterprise.

- The rich have traditionally exploited the poor, partly by dividing them against one another. If poor people join together they can empower themselves to achieve social and political as well as economic goals.

7. Ask participants to describe group enterprises from their own experience, or about which they have heard, which have succeeded. Are there any common features from which we can learn?

Summarize participants' observations on the board. Some of them may be restatements of the lessons from the Basket Makers' Society case study. They may include points such as:

- People should do what they want to do. No form of enterprise should be forced on them.

- The members should have a shared common need.

- A group enterprise has to be viable and well-managed like any other form of business.

- Group enterprises with one quite simple function – such as milk collection, or fertilizer distribution, or crop marketing, or savings mobilization – are more likely to succeed than complex businesses.

- Group enterprises must be allowed to fail, like any other.

8. Stress, in conclusion, that there are no rules as to when group enterprises are and are not appropriate. People must be free to make their own decisions, and the role of the NGO should be to show people the options that are available and to facilitate their doing what they want to do.

NGO staff should *not* promote group enterprises because they believe that they are the only 'correct' form of business, or because they are more convenient for the NGO to assist.

DAY FIVE — SESSION ONE

The Basket Makers' Society

The people of village X had always made baskets, and they seemed always to have been very poor. Simon, the field-worker for the ABC NGO, was therefore very happy when he organized them into a society in order to improve their situation.

Middlemen from outside the village used to deliver material to the people and then take away the finished baskets. Some of the village people had seen the baskets on sale in the nearby market and they knew that the middlemen made an enormous profit. Simon explained to them that they would be able to earn all that extra money themselves, and he also told them that the ABC NGO would be able to help them with special grants if they formed a society. They had then been very happy to form a society as he suggested.

Simon had been particularly pleased that so many of the village people had joined; one or two rather richer men who owned some land around the village had also joined. National elections were due shortly, and Simon was delighted when a local politician had also promised his support.

Simon knew that the people were very skilled and that their baskets could be sold in great quantities and for high prices, if certain changes were made. They needed different grades of material and a wider range of designs. He also suggested that they should try to sell their baskets in the city and to some exporters. They would need extra finance for this, and Simon put them in touch with the nearby co-operative bank.

The people had elected a committee, and they had appointed one of the more-educated members to be manager. Simon made frequent visits to the village, however, and he acted as an informal part-time manager for the new society. Their manager inevitably made some serious mistakes, and the society ran out of money more than once. But Simon was able to provide grants for them from the ABC NGO emergency fund, so that they survived.

The society had been going for about a year, and Simon was convinced that he had done everything he could for the members. He was therefore very surprised and disappointed when he went to the village for one of his visits and found that the society seemed to have collapsed. He heard various stories from various members, but it was clear that there had been some major disagreements, and nobody seemed to know where the money had gone. They were all clear on one thing, however: the society had failed, and some of the people had already started buying materials from the middlemen again.

ASSIGNMENT

What mistakes did Simon and the ABC NGO make?

Group enterprises — when and how?

OBJECTIVE
To enable participants to identify situations when group enterprise may be appropriate, and to assist them effectively.

TIME
One to one and a half hours.

MATERIALS

The Shantyburg Women's Groups, case-study.

SESSION GUIDE

1. Remind participants of the previous session. Group enterprises are not always the best way for people to run businesses. NGOs can often do more harm than good by promoting groups when they are not appropriate, or by misdirected assistance to them when they are.

We should not discard the whole concept of groups because it has been to some extent discredited by government and even by NGOs. The objective of this session is to help us identify the types of activities when groups are effective, and then to assist them in such a way as to help and not destroy them.

2. Many NGOs themselves fund and effectively manage activities in communities. If the NGO is to be able to withdraw, then these activities must be owned and managed by somebody else. It is not always possible to start an activity under genuine community ownership and management. NGOs often fail even to try because of the urgency of the need which the activity is set up to satisfy, or because there is nobody in the community with the necessary skills to manage it.

Ask participants to suggest examples of such activities; put together a list including the following, but omit the P and G at this point:

A savings and credit programme.	G
A vehicle to transport people, crops and farm supplies.	P
A well or other irrigation scheme to serve small farmers.	G
A storage shed.	P
A crèche.	G
A retail shop to sell handicrafts.	P
A raw-material supply service.	G
A tractor or threshing service for the farmers.	P

Ask participants to imagine that their NGOs have set up these enterprises, and must now withdraw. Allow them up to ten minutes to decide which of these activities, all things being equal, would best be taken over by a community or group enterprise, and which would best be owned and managed as private businesses.

3. Ask for their suggestions. Clearly there are no hard and fast rules, and each decision should be taken on its merits, in consultation with the community. The right-hand column of G for group and P for private represents one set of opinions. Hold brief discussion on each case, and evolve a list of criteria which favour group, or private enterprises.

This might include the following. Group enterprises may be best when:

- It is difficult to make individual charges for the service.

- The activity does not require full-time management.

- All the members have a vital personal interest in the service.

- The activity does not require fast decisions.

- The task is fairly risk-free.

Private enterprises may be best when:

- There are likely to be competitive suppliers, to prevent exploitation.

- The activity needs instant decisions on issues such as prices.

- The community will not all benefit equally from the service.

- The activity involves high risks.

- The activity demands very hard continuous commitment.

- The activity is one where it is difficult to share the work.

Remind participants that the choice should of course rest with the community. Nevertheless, an NGO must be ready to advise its clients, and such advice should be given not on the basis of any prejudice or ideological preference, but on a realistic assessment of what will be best for the people.

4. Distribute the hand-out, The Shantyburg Women's Groups. Allow participants up to 20 minutes to read it. If time allows, they may then discuss it in groups, or they can be asked for their individual views.

The case-study can be interpreted in many different ways. Encourage discussion, and list suggestions such as:

- NGOs should avoid giving gifts to anyone, since this 'pollutes' people's motives for participating in any future activities the NGO may undertake.

- Even matching grants can be dangerous. People can never have the same sense of responsibility for money which is not their own.

- The best policy for an outside change agent is often to float ideas and then to leave people to do what they want to do. Too much follow-up can be worse than too little.

- People should be allowed to sort out their own problems whenever possible. Any intervention to exclude Mrs A would in fact have been disastrous.

5. The case study showed how groups can be very effective indeed, and participants should have many similar examples. Groups are like sensitive plants, however. It is very easy to starve them but they can also be killed by over-feeding. It is important

for outsiders to understand the processes involved in group formation, in order to know how to intervene, or not to intervene, at the different stages of group development.

It is unlikely that any of the enterprise experiences have been organized on a group basis, perhaps because the participants were not well-acquainted with one another when the course started, or because people's natural preference is to work on their own. Ask participants to imagine that one of them has suggested that they themselves, as a group, should now undertake some activity such as organizing an evening's entertainment. What stages would the group go through, in terms of its own development, before it would start to perform the task?

Participants may find it difficult to imagine what would happen. Ask them to recall any similar occasion when they have been members of a group. What stages did that group go through?

Most groups typically go through the following stages:

a. The group comes together, usually with great enthusiasm (forming).

b. The members disagree over the activities and responsibilities, and some may drop out (storming).

c. The surviving members agree on office bearers, and on procedures and norms, which limit disagreements and other problems (norming).

d. The group starts to undertake the actual tasks it was set up to carry out (performing).

6. Ask participants to suggest what types of intervention, if any, are appropriate at each of the four stages of this process of 'forming, storming, norming and performing'. Ask them to support their suggestions by reference to their own experiences. Encourage suggestions such as:

a. During 'forming', outsiders should limit their intervention to suggesting (but not aggressively promoting or financially rewarding) the idea for the group to form. Members must be able to choose or reject their own fellow members.

b. During 'storming' outsiders should keep away, and should not in any way try to persuade hesitant members to remain or to resolve outstanding issues for the group. It is up to them, and it is better to allow a group to fail at this stage, than 'artificially' to keep it alive so that it fails later when far more is at stake.

c. During 'norming' outsiders can help with advice on procedures, responsibilities and regulations. The outsider must only advise and not take over, but he can offer valuable advice at this stage, when the group is ready to regularize its affairs.

d. Once a group is performing, it should be strong enough to make use of outside assistance without being taken over. The three earlier stages, and particularly the 'storming', may be necessary for the establishment of a strong group.

7. Summarize the session by stressing the most important skill in developing groups for enterprise may be to know when not to intervene. Paradoxically, the most successful groups are often the ones which have received the least assistance.

DAY FIVE — SESSION TWO

The Shantyburg Women's Groups

Shantyburg is a slum settlement on the outskirts of Cityville. It was settled in the late 1980s by some 10 000 squatters who had been expelled from the city. They came from various parts of the country, and had been living in slum settlements in Cityville. They were involved in outbreaks of violence and disorder; the authorities shifted them out of the city, and allocated an area of land for their resettlement. Each family was allocated a small plot, stand-pipes were provided and electricity was made available; the people were also given some building materials to help them construct their houses. The settlement was called Shantyburg, because it remained half built.

The people remained poor, and although their housing was a little better than their old slums they were now far away from the city where they had earned their living by petty trading, begging, prostitution and other means. A number of NGOs attempted to provide some assistance, but there was no real sense of community and many programmes failed because of communal jealousies.

Mr X, a foreigner who was working in Cityville, had visited Shantyburg and had given some money to one or two of the poorest families who were in desperate need. In March 1992 he was about to return to Europe, and on his last visit to Shantyburg a large number of poor women crowded round him, asking for money. He realised that he could not help them all, and that they needed to help themselves. He therefore suggested that they should try to start regular saving, in groups. He explained how women in many other places had been able to increase their incomes by starting small group loan funds from their regular savings, and he said that he would be happy to match their own savings when he next came to Cityville, provided they could show that they had been saving regularly, and that they deposited their savings in a joint account in a bank or post office.

Mr X came back to Shantyburg in August 1992 and found that the women had started two groups. The leaders of one group proudly showed their post office savings bank passbook with a credit balance of $55, made up of five deposits of $11 each, being their monthly savings at a rate of fifty cents for each of the 22 members. Mr X was very pleased, and he gave them another $55 in cash. They agreed that they would deposit this in the post office and continue their own savings. They agreed also to discuss how to start lending to the members from the fund.

Some members of the other group told him about their experience. They said that 36 members had joined, under the leadership of Mrs A, a woman who lived in Shantyburg but had had some education. She was a part-time social worker for one of the NGOs, and could speak some English. Mr X had met her on some of her previous visits to Shantyburg, and had commissioned her to undertake some research survey work, but she was not there on this occasion.

The members of her group said that they had been saving fifty cents a month, but they did not know anything about where the money was or how much they had accumulated; some of them said that they suspected Mrs A had stolen it. Mr X was very disappointed; he said that he would probably be coming again early in 1993, and hoped they would be able to give some better news then.

In February 1993 Mr X he went to Shantyburg again. He met Mrs A. She apologised for not being available when Mr X was there the previous August, but showed him a passbook in the joint names of herself and another member; there was a single entry of $150, in January 1993. Mrs A explained that she had initially been depositing the savings in a passbook account at the bank, in her own name, since the bank would not permit unregistered groups to open accounts. In January she had shifted the money to a joint account at the post office, because some of the group members complained that she was keeping the money for herself.

She said that the 36 members had been saving fifty cents a month more or less regularly and they now wanted to know what to do next. She clearly hoped that Mr X would match the money they had saved, but he did not have the necessary cash and was in any case a little unsure about what was really happening in the group. He was not sure what to do.

Mr X then talked to some of the members of the other group, to whom he had given $55 the previous August. They had a sad tale to tell; apparently the group had started to argue and even to fight immediately after Mr X had given them the money. After a few days they had decided to break up the group; they had eventually agreed to withdraw the money and to divide it up among themselves, and to disband the group. The two women who were the signatories decided to leave $1 each in the account, in the hope that they might start again, and they sadly showed Mr X the passbook. He wondered what mistakes he had made, and what he should say to the women.

Mr X made a further visit to Shantyburg in February 1994. He met some of the women from the first group, and they said they had never succeeded in starting again; too much ill will had been generated when it broke up.

Mr X also met some of the members of the second group, although Mrs A was again not there. They showed him their records; the 36 members had each saved $11.50, or fifty cents for each of the 23 months since Mr X had originally suggested the idea. They had also started lending money from their group fund to one another as Mr X had suggested; they had decided to charge themselves three cents per dollar for each month, and their total fund now amounted to $504 in cash, savings and outstanding loans. This included their total savings of 36 times $11.50, or $414, and a further $90 of accumulated interest from the loans they had made to one another from their fund.

Assignment

What does this experience tell us about the ways in which outsiders, such as NGOs or well-intentioned foreigners, should and should not promote groups?

Introduction to marketing

OBJECTIVE

To enable participants to identify ways in which the products and services of poor people's enterprises are marketed, in order to be able to assist and advise their clients to market their goods and services more effectively.

TIME

One to one and a half hours.

SESSION GUIDE

1. Ask participants to recall a recent purchase which they made. It might be something quite trivial, such as a tube of toothpaste, a packet of cigarettes or a newspaper; or it might be something more important such as a car, an item of clothing or a gift.

Ask them to think carefully about why they bought that particular item, from that place. There are almost always many different providers of the products or services we need. What was the most important reason that they chose that particular product, from that place?

You should now use the reasons participants have given in order to lead participants to 'discover' for themselves the principle of the 'marketing mix' of the 'four Ps': price, product, place and promotion.

Divide the board into four quadrants. Allocate one quadrant to each of the four Ps, in your mind, but do not at this stage state or write any titles in each quadrant. The purpose is to let the participants discover this for themselves.

Go round the class, asking participants in turn to say what he bought and why. Write a brief note of each item, and the reason for its purchase, in the appropriate quadrant, in the following form:

Price	*Product*
Car – best price	A meal – best quality
Shoes – cheapest of that type	Shirt – the best brand
Place	*Promotion*
Toothpaste – only shop open	Cinema – it was advertised
Newspaper – delivered to home	Cold drink – saw the stall

2. Continue until there are at least two entries for each quadrant. If one or more of the quadrants are empty, you may yourself fill the gap by describing a purchase you yourself made recently, and asking participants to suggest why you purchased that product at that place. Or you may ask participants to think of another purchase,

90

perhaps suggesting a product for which the purchase reason is likely to fill the empty gap.

When all the participants' purchases and reasons have been listed. Or, if the pace is dragging, when there is at least one entry in each quadrant, ask participants to try to explain why you have allocated them into the four quadrants, which are at that stage unlabelled. Elicit the conclusion that you have put together reasons of a particular type, and that the all the reasons in a particular quadrant can, loosely at any rate, be defined under the particular 'P' to which you have allocated it. Then label each quadrant with the appropriate 'P'.

Explain that people's reasons for purchases, and thus the motives to which suppliers must try to appeal if they are to succeed, can loosely be divided into these 'four Ps'. This simple classification provides a useful tool for deciding how to market any product or service.

3. It is probable that the majority of the reasons will fall into the 'price' or the 'product' quadrants, but it is important that participants should recognize that they, and thus their clients' customers too, actually buy things according to a far more complex mix of reasons than we ourselves often recognize. Successful businesses put together a marketing mix in the right proportion of each of the 'four Ps' to suit the needs and tastes of their potential customers.

Ask participants to think about the clothes they are wearing right now, in the classroom. Why did they choose those particular items? Some may refer to the low price or the durability of a particular piece of clothing. Ask them whether that particular shirt or dress is in fact the cheapest and most durable way of achieving the basic needs for warmth and decency which are satisfied by clothes.

Seek the response that they are almost certainly not. A plain empty cloth bag with three holes cut in the top would satisfy these needs just as well, and perhaps better and more conveniently than some clothes, and certainly far more cheaply. How many participants actually use their clothes until they are worn out?

Participants should realize that when we buy clothes – and many if not most other things – we are in fact 'buying' a whole mix of attributes, which go far beyond the physical product itself:

• We are buying beauty and attractiveness.

• We may 'buy' the pleasure of making purchases from a particular shop.

• We are making a statement about ourselves to the world.

• We are confirming our opinion of ourselves to ourselves.

4. Confirm participants' understanding of the idea of the 'marketing mix' by referring to the four quadrants on the board. Ask someone who purchased a fairly expensive item such as a scooter or large home appliance whether he would have been prepared to travel a few kilometres to save ten per cent. Would someone who bought a newspaper or packet of cigarettes have been willing to do the same for a saving on that item? Clearly not; the marketing mix is designed to satisfy the most important needs involved in each type of purchase. The mix for small 'convenience' items concentrates on the 'P' of place, while suppliers of more expensive items have to think more about the price 'P'. List a few familiar items; ask participants which 'P' is most important for each of them?

- Newspaper – place (which includes time).

- TV set – product and price and promotion, a known brand.

- Cold drink – place and promotion.

- Clothing – product.

- Rice and other staple foods – price (for a given quality).

Show by examples how a producer can vary the 'mix' for different circumstances and customers. Some people are willing or able to travel a long way to save money, while others may have to buy locally and pay more. Some people insist on a certain brand while others will buy any brand, or unbranded products, to save money.

Remind participants that the same principle applies equally to services such as banks, insurance or transport. Everyone, including an NGO providing enterprise development services to the poor, has to design a 'marketing mix' which suits the needs of his clients.

5. Remind participants of their enterprise experiences; ask them to say which of the 'four Ps' they used to market their goods or services. Typical examples might include:

- Snack food items – Product quality and Promotion.

- Laundry services – Place.

- Photographic services – Place and Promotion.

- Evening entertainment – Place and Product quality.

- Weekend outing – Product and Price.

Ask participants to think about some of the products on which their clients spend money. Everyone spends money on 'non-essential items', and price is a less important reason for purchase, by poor customers as well as richer ones, than we commonly suppose.

Ask participants to mention some famous brand names of products which seem to have a dominating share of their markets. Encourage examples like:

- Datsun for cars.

- Colgate for toothpaste.

- Omo for washing powder.

- Coca-cola for carbonated drinks.

- Aspro for aspirins.

Ask whether these are the cheapest products of their kind on the market; generally they are not. Successful businesses are those which market their goods effectively. This usually involves spending more money than competitors on product quality and on items such as promotion, packaging and brand names rather than making the product as cheaply as possible.

Ask for an example of a local small business which is known to them and has gained a major share of its market. Discuss the reasons for its success, and analyse it in terms of the marketing mix. It is unlikely to be the lowest-cost supplier, even if its customers are poor people.

People with very little money often choose not to buy from the cheapest shops. Discuss why this is so, and guide participants to the conclusion that marketing is about adding value, not cutting prices.

6. Ask participants whether micro-enterprises such as those which NGOs assist their clients to operate can market their products or services by adding value rather than cutting prices. Is this an advantage which only the large national or international companies can benefit from, or do smaller businesses enjoy some advantages which their larger competitors do not?

List micro-enterprise advantages such as:

- They can offer tailor-made products and services.

- They operate locally, near to their customers.

- They owners can make fast decisions, on the spot.

- They can offer round-the-clock service.

- Their customers can negotiate directly with the owner.

Remind participants that entrepreneurs are people who see opportunities where others see problems, and marketing is perhaps the best test of enterprise. NGOs should be aware of the market advantages of their clients' businesses, and encourage clients to exploit them.

Marketing applications

OBJECTIVE
To enable participants to apply their knowledge of marketing to real situations.

TIME
One and a half to two hours.

MATERIALS

These 'Marketing Micro-cases', like all the case-studies in the material, should be amended to include examples of the kinds of businesses with which participants are likely to be most concerned.

Participants should also be asked to bring to this session the material they presented the previous day on the businesses they had visited.

SESSION GUIDE

1. Ask a participant to remind the group about the 'four Ps'. During this session they will have an opportunity to see how the marketing tools which have been developed by large-scale manufacturers of cold drinks, aspirins or toothpaste, or by themselves for their own enterprise experiences, can be and are applied by poor people for their own businesses.

Distribute copies of the 'Marketing Micro-cases'. Allow participants five minutes to think of as many suggestions as they can for the shoeshine man in the first example. They can use the concept of the 'four Ps' to think about the present situation of each example and to identify ways that the people in question can add value by marketing innovations.

Remind them of the earlier 'brainstorming' exercise when they were trying to convert problems into opportunities. This is a similar exercise, but with a marketing slant. Ask round the class for suggestions, and do not allow any idea to be dismissed out of hand. List the possibilities such as:

- He can sell shoelaces, shoe polish and brushes to his customers.

- He can offer a shoe-dyeing service for customers who want to change the colour of their shoes.

- He can offer a shoe repair service.

- He can offer slippers on loan to customers who are in a hurry, so that they can complete their shopping while he cleans their shoes.

Demonstrate that these and similar suggestions arise from considering the customers' needs and how they can be satisfied. This is the essence of successful marketing, for any business. Do not put forward the above suggestions as the 'right' answers, but use them to encourage ideas from participants. All these ideas, like those for the other three examples which follow, are currently being successfully implemented by micro-enterprises which faced the problems described in the case-studies.

2. Allow a further five minutes for the second case, the wood carvers. List suggestions such as:

- Encourage tourists to visit the carvers in the village and to see the carving being made. Sell them simple refreshments and the carving.
- Make new products such as furniture which incorporate the traditional designs.
- Negotiate to set up a carving demonstration in an hotel lobby or elsewhere in the tourist area, and sell carvings to people who come to see it.

Many governments, and NGOs, believe that traditional handicraft skills can only be preserved through protection or subsidy, rather than by innovation. This usually fails, or can only benefit a small number of products. The above are modest examples, which have all been done by craftsmen in various parts of the world, of ways in which traditional producers can compete in the modern market-place.

3. Do the same with the third case, that of the fruit-sellers. Encourage suggestions such as:

- Get together and rent a vehicle to take the fruit to the town and sell it there for higher prices.
- Get together and make an arrangement with the factory buyer to collect the right quantity of fruit for him in advance, at a predetermined price, to save him time.
- Identify other similar factories and offer to provide the same service for them.

These and other suggestions require group action. Stress that small producers often have to work together to develop links and market their goods, but that they will only succeed if they offer an extra service to their customers. Purely protective group action, with no improvement in marketing, is unlikely to succeed.

4. Do the same for the fourth case, that of the tailor. List suggestions such as:

- Start to make a few ready-made garments herself, in her spare time.
- Make an arrangement with a local clothing shop to make alterations for ready-made garments which are not a good fit.
- Buy, repair and resell second-hand clothing.

Show that nearly every type of business has evolved from earlier businesses which have been 'destroyed' by new tastes, new technologies or new ideas. Cars destroyed horse-drawn carriages but created a vast market for new micro-enterprises such as roadside repair services and car cleaners as well as for large oil companies, car manufacturers and so on. Some of the older businesses respond to changes by treating them as opportunities, like the above examples. Others treat them only as threats and problems, and are eventually destroyed.

5. Ask the sub-groups from the previous day's business presentations to apply the 'four Ps' concept to the business they studied, and to identify some ways in which their owners could improve their marketing. The recommendations they made in the

earlier session may have been for marketing improvements. This session will give them an opportunity to refine and add to what they proposed then, in the light of what they have learned about marketing.

Remind participants that 'product' is one of the 'four Ps'. It is impossible and wrong to try to separate marketing from the business as a whole. The critical difference between selling and marketing is that selling is just about how to persuade people to buy the products you have, in the place and at the price that you have decided. Marketing covers the whole way the business relates to its customers, who are of course the reason why the business exists at all.

6. Ask a representative from each sub-group to state briefly what marketing improvements they have identified, showing which 'P' or combination of 'Ps' they relate to. Stress that the 'four Ps' is only a concept, which they should use or discard depending on whether they find it valuable or not; it is not something which should be learned and applied for its own sake.

If time allows, introduce other marketing concepts:

- Market segmentation, which means identifying a particular type of purchaser, and targeting the 'mix' at them. The person who needs more than just a shoeshine, or the factory fruit-buyer, are examples of specialized market segments.

- The choice between selling more of the same products to new customers, like the tourists buying carvings, and selling new products to existing customers, like shoe-laces or repairs to people who have their shoes shined.

7. Some participants may feel that marketing is in some way unethical, in that it usually involves selling products for more than their physical cost. Show that good marketing is a way of adding value to people's labour. A day labourer only earns the minimum price for his time and effort, while his employer collects the value added by marketing. NGOs should help their clients to market their products better, so that they too will add value to their labour.

8. Remind participants that they should not only understand and assist their clients to market their products and services more effectively; but they must themselves market the services of their NGOs.

Ask whether the concepts of the 'four Ps' and the marketing mix can be applied to an NGO. How can an NGO use these concepts to improve its services to its clients? Help them to come up with the following:

- The product of an NGO is its services, which must be designed in such a way as genuinely to address the needs of its clients.

- The place where an NGO offers its services is vital. It must reach out to the community, so that it can serve its clients where and when they need the service.

- An NGO must promote its services in order to inform its clients, and its donors, about what it offers. The best services are useless if the clients for whom they are intended do not know about them, or do not understand them.

- Even if clients do not have to pay for an NGO's services, they have to spend time and perhaps money on travel, be absent from work and lose earning opportunities.

Marketing can be misused to exploit people's ignorance and to create 'artificial' needs. Participants should not complain that soft drinks, cigarettes and other extravagant and not particularly desirable products are so effectively marketed, even to poor people. NGOs should learn from successful commercial marketing in order to satisfy their clients' real needs more effectively and efficiently.

Marketing micro-cases

Here are four very brief accounts of micro-enterprises which have problems; read each one, and come up with some practical but imaginative and creative suggestions as to how each business might improve its sales by better marketing.

Abdul the shoe cleaner

Abdul is a 'shoeshine boy'; he sits on the pavement of a busy city street where many business people walk by. He asks people whose shoes are not clean, and who look able to afford to have their shoes polished, to use his services and his business earns him just enough to keep him and his family alive.

He has lots of problems though; sometimes his client's shoes are damaged so that he cannot clean them properly and once he broke a customer's shoe laces when he was tying them up after cleaning the shoes; even rich people seem to have very worn-out shoe laces. He says that in the 'good old days' people would take care of their shoes, and they were always black or brown. Now shoes seem to be a fashion item, and people want to change the colours of their shoes just like their ties. Abdul is afraid his business will die out unless he can get more business.

The Templeton Woodcarvers

Templeton is a small town which is internationally famous for its old stone temples; people come from all over the world to see them. The city used to be famous for its wooden carvings too, but now there is only one small woodcarvers' village near the town. The patterns are similar to those carved on the temples, but tourists buy modern souvenirs and seem to have no interest in the traditional handicrafts.

The village lies a few hundred metres from the temples, just off the main road, but the tourists do not see it. They get out of their buses and look at the temples, they buy snacks and souvenirs from the cluster of shops that has sprung up, and then they leave. The woodcarvers sell less and less of their work, mainly to the State Board and some traders who know the place and buy the wooden carvings for shops in the cities or even abroad. The woodcarvers think that in one or two generations there will be none of them at all left in Templetown.

The friendly fruit-sellers

The women in the community have traditionally sold the fruit grown on their farms. They carry it to the local market where traders come and buy it for consumption and processing in the city. It is excellent fruit, and there is a big demand, but the traders have always seen to it that the women only get low prices.

A new processing factory has recently opened about 50km away, and the buyer comes to the market every week to buy fruit. The women have always had to bargain hard with the traders and they do the same with the factory buyer. He buys large quantities, and pays cash, so he gets low prices. He complains, however, about having to spend half a day going round the market, arguing with each woman, before he has what he needs. He says that 'time is money' nowadays.

The women sit round the tree in the market in the evenings, after the buyers have gone. They know and trust one another, and they know that they all sell for about the same price in the end. They wish they could find a way of earning more money from their business.

Tara the tailor

Tara is a skilled tailor. She has a small place near the town centre, where she makes men's and women's garments from the cloth her customers bring her. She is also good at repair work.

She is worried though, because she knows that people are going more and more for ready-made garments, or even for second-hand clothing which is now available from several stalls in the market. She has heard people complaining that ready-made clothes do not always fit properly, and second-hand garments are often in a poor state of repair, but customers seem to want to see the thing they are buying before they decide to buy it. Tara could never even begin to rival the range of items which the big shops offer in the town.

Quality and efficiency

OBJECTIVE

To enable participants to recognize poor quality and inefficiency in their own or others' work; to recognize the reasons for them and their dangers; and to identify ways in which they can improve the quality and efficiency of their own work.

TIME

One hour.

MATERIAL AND ADVANCE PREPARATION

Bring to the class a cake of locally made soap, and a similar sized piece of a nationally advertised and branded soap. Also bring some examples of good- and of bad-quality products made by local informal businesses, such as handicrafts, garments or simple kitchen tools or vessels, or ask participants to bring some typical examples of products produced by their clients.

SESSION GUIDE

1. Ask participants to look around the classroom in which they are sitting, at the walls, the ceiling, the floor and the furniture. What comments do they have on the quality of what they see?

If they can see nothing they consider worth commenting on, draw their attention to a particular detail, such as the finish of the chairs they are sitting on, the way in which a window frame has been painted or the way in which a certain light switch is fixed to the wall.

Ask for specific comments on the details of the way in which the job has been done, such as:

- The wood or metal parts of the chairs are roughly cut and not properly finished.

- The paint is splattered on the window glass and some parts of the bare wood are unpainted.

- The switch is crooked, or the switch box is not fixed tightly to the wall.

2. Ask participants to suggest why such minor details are important. Call for suggestions such as:

- They are wasteful; the wood may rot; the daylight will be excluded.

- They may be dangerous; they may cause electric shocks or fires or tear clothing.

Ask participants to explain these examples of poor quality. Why were the jobs not done properly?

- The person who did the job was not skilled, or he did not take pride in doing the job well. He just did the minimum that was acceptable.

100

- The manager who was responsible for quality control, and the client who was paying for the job to be done, did not pay attention to such small details.

Participants may suggest that such low quality can be explained by the fact that the job was done as cheaply as possible. The institution could not afford to pay for better quality, and the contractor could not afford to pay for more skilled workers or better supervision.

Ask whether low quality of this sort is really economical. Are things which have been built and finished in this way more durable and efficient than those that are built to higher standards?

Clearly they are not; poor quality is not the result of poverty, but is a cause of poverty. Stress that poor quality of this sort is wasteful, and expensive in the long run. Such problems may also explain why countries where wages are ten or even a hundred times higher than in 'developing countries' can still compete successfully, because of the high quality of their products and the efficiency with which they are made.

3. Ask participants to think self-critically about their own working environment and the way they do their jobs. Can they mention similar low-quality work for which they are responsible?

Request examples by asking participants to think about the appearance of their own offices in the same way as they have just looked at the classroom. Are there piles of unsorted papers lying about, is the floor clean?

They should also think about letters or papers they may have been working with recently. Were there uncorrected errors in the typing? Are reports laid out clearly and presented at the proper time?

4. After some participants have mentioned such examples, ask them to suggest why they matter. Is it not better quickly to correct by hand mistakes in letters and not to waste time cleaning offices or sorting papers? What is wrong with poor quality of this kind, so long as the report or the letter can be read?

Look for the response that low quality in such small matters leads to low quality in more important things. What is likely to be the influence of a badly typed letter on:

- The timeliness of the attendance of somebody whom the letter is asking to a meeting.
- The opinion of the reader about the writer's application for funding which the letter contains.
- The repayment performance of the recipient of a letter asking him to repay his overdue loan instalment.

An untidy office or badly kept records can have a similar effect, not only on clients and colleagues, but on the person who occupies the office or keeps the records. Low quality is 'infectious', it spreads within a person's work and between people and institutions.

5. Ask participants to compare the quality of the local soap with international brands of soap. Why do many people prefer to buy the branded soap even though

it is much more expensive? Elicit comments on the convenience, the packaging, the perfume and the general quality of the branded soap. People are willing to pay extra for quality.

This example may imply that local products must always be of lower quality and sell for lower prices, than products which have been mass produced by large companies. Ask participants whether products made locally by micro-enterprises such as their clients can compete with factory-made products on quality.

6. Hand round some good examples of local handicrafts such as woven cloth, bamboo or grass-fibre baskets or wood carvings. Ask participants to recall the working and living environment of rural poor people they work with. How do these products, and the environment in which they are made, differ from the 'modern' products and environment as represented by the classroom, or participants' own offices and 'products' such as reports and letters?

Guide the group towards the response that the traditional products, and the homes and workshops of the rural craftspeople who made them, are usually of a higher quality than more 'modern' products. They are also better quality than the environment and 'products' of our own 'modern' institutions as well.

7. Ask participants to discuss how these traditional high quality standards can be preserved and expanded rather than lost in the search for higher incomes through new enterprise. Lead participants to conclude that:

- They should themselves respect and learn from their clients, and thus improve the quality of what their own NGOs do.

- They should demand high quality from client enterprises when they are buying from them or training or advising them. Once a producer believes that low quality is acceptable, it is very difficult to improve his standards.

8. Ask each participant to spend five minutes thinking at once about and writing down *one* quality improvement that she can make at once to her own work. This may be something very modest, relating perhaps to the notes she is taking on the course, the presentation of a particular report or a detail of her office or the records she keeps.

Allow each participant a maximum of one minute to state what she proposes to do, and make a note on the board of each 'quality commitment' so that you and the group as a whole can monitor their implementation. Stress that bad quality is infectious and can be a habit, but so is good quality. All participants should start now to cultivate a habit of good quality.

Record keeping

OBJECTIVE
To enable participants to identify and recommend appropriate forms of record keeping for literate and illiterate owners of micro-enterprises.

TIME
One and a half to two and a half hours.

ADVANCE PREPARATION

Participants should be asked before this session to prepare and submit current balance sheets for their enterprise experience businesses, together with profit and loss accounts for operations to date. The instructor should go through them before the session to identify common errors, which can be discussed at the end of this session without revealing the details of the results of each business. The accounts should be handed back to the participants who have prepared them, with a note of any errors. These can also be explained to them individually, in order to ensure that they are corrected before the preparation of the final results.

SESSION GUIDE

1. Ask participants whether it is necessary for the owners of businesses to keep business records. Some, if not all, will answer that it is. Ask them whether the owners of most micro-businesses are able to read and write. Elicit the answer that they are not, particularly the women who make up the majority of such people. This demonstrates that it is possible to run a micro-enterprise without any written records, since so many millions of people do.

Ask participants if they know of any illiterate millionaires. Stress that there are many of them, in Europe and North America as well as in developing countries. Literacy can help people to run their businesses better, but there are many much more important success factors such as hard work, creativity, determination and shrewd judgement.

2. Ask any participants who are involved in training people for self-employment whether they include bookkeeping in their courses. Ask one who does why he includes it, and what his trainees actually gain from the knowledge they acquire, in terms of higher earnings.

Stress that keeping business records is in itself a cost; the business person has to buy the pen and the paper, and, far more important, she has to spend *time* on writing down the figures. People without good education often take a very long time to keep even quite simple records, and they often make simple arithmetical mistakes which make the records totally misleading.

The time and money that people invest in keeping records must earn a return, like any other business investment. This will only happen if the records are *used*, and most small business management training courses fail to teach people how to use their accounts, and many do not even try to teach them this.

3. Ask participants why it is that so many small business management courses include business record-keeping, when so few of the trainees actually use what they learn and thus earn a return on the time and effort they put into keeping records. Encourage answers such as:

- Most business management textbooks and formal courses relate to bigger formal businesses, whose staff can keep and use records. We have usually learned from such books and courses, and we teach what we have learned.

- It is relatively easy for people who have never been in business to teach others to keep records. It is very difficult to teach less 'formal' but more useful things.

- It is easy to find out if we have succeeded in teaching people how to keep records. We can set a test, or visit them in their businesses and inspect the records. It is far more difficult to evaluate other lessons.

- We may want to be able to assess businesses for evaluation or loan approval purposes. We teach them to keep records for our sake, not for their own.

4. We often say that business people should keep records, as if that in itself will improve their businesses. Records are only tools which some people need to solve problems.

Write the following brief business problems on the board. Allow participants up to ten minutes to decide how they might advise a literate business person to solve them:

a. A small shopkeeper finds that he often runs out of stocks, because he forgets to order new goods in time.

b. A shoemaker wants to know how much he should draw from his business every month, and how to prevent himself from exceeding the limit.

c. A tea-shop owner has to sell on credit in order to compete, but she finds it difficult to remember how much each customer owes her.

5. Ask them for their suggestions. They might be as follows:

a. The shopkeeper should make up a simple 'bin card' for each item of stock. He should note down the quantities that he receives and that he sells, and the balance, and should also note on the top of the card the number at which he should restock, allowing for delays in delivery. When the balance reaches this 're-order' figure, he should do so.

b. The shoemaker should record every transaction for one or two months, as illustrated in the 'dynamic balance sheet' session. He should then calculate his profits, and, depending on his needs and future plans, he should set a wage for himself which allows for reinvestment. He should draw this amount every day, week or month, as appropriate.

c. The tea-shop owner should draw up a credit record page or card for each customer on the same basis as the 'bin card', with columns for the date, credit given, cash paid, the balance and a signature or thumb print for the customer to acknowledge each transaction. She should also make a note on the card of the maximum amount of credit she thinks that customer should be allowed to have. She should record each credit sale or cash payment as it takes place, and also calculate the balance, so that she can stop giving credit when it reaches the limit, and also tell each customer how much he owes whenever he makes a purchase.

6. Now divide the participants into small groups and ask them to perform the same assignment again, but this time to assume that the people described are totally illiterate. They should be ready to describe their 'systems' and also actually to demonstrate the system with any materials they have to hand. This is clearly a far more difficult task than the first assignment. Some participants may even object that it is impossible.

People who are literate find it difficult to put themselves in the position of those who are not. Some participants may make the mistake of assuming that people who are illiterate are stupid, or cannot count. Remind them of the millions of illiterate people who successfully manage micro-enterprises all over the world. If they are really to be able to assist micro-business people they must be able to understand and work with the vast majority who are illiterate.

Remind them that the best teachers are often the owners of micro-enterprises themselves. They should think of business people they know, such as those whom they interviewed earlier in the course, and try to remember how they kept track of important aspects of their businesses.

7. Allow between 30 minutes and one hour for this task. Reconvene the class, and ask a representative of each group briefly to describe and to demonstrate what they suggest. Encourage discussion, and ensure that the suggestions are understandable and effective; there is a large range of possibilities, but typical systems might be as follows:

a. Stock reordering times and quantities can be assessed by making a chalk mark on the shelf or floor where the goods are stored, to mark the point at which the number has fallen to the 'reorder point'. The mark will be uncovered when the number falls to that quantity, and this will show the shopkeeper that he must now restock. He should of course move the items at the back of the shelf to the front when the new stocks are put on the shelf, to prevent accumulation of old stocks.

b. The shoemaker should estimate his profits over a day, a week or a month as appropriate by simply counting the money he has at the start and comparing this with what he has at the end of the period. He should then decide what should be his wage, based not on what he thinks he 'should' earn but as a proportion of the profits, allowing for expansion and for bad periods. He should then put an appropriate number of pebbles in a tin or pieces of paper on a spike, one for each ten cents, or one or ten dollars as is appropriate, and should remove a pebble or tear off a piece of paper each time he takes that amount of money from the business. When the tin or the spike is empty, he should not withdraw any more money until the next period.

c. If there is strong mutual trust between the woman and her credit customers, the woman might keep a page in a notebook or a card for each customer, identified with a drawing or other indicator of that particular person. She would then make a mark on the page for each ten cents or dollar of credit, and then cross out the appropriate number of marks when cash payments were made. The 'balance' of marks not crossed out would be the balance unpaid.

105

If there was any possibility of disagreement or mistrust, she might herself buy, or sell to each credit customer, a small box which can be locked with a key. She would mark the boxes to show which belonged to each customer, and would then give the keys to the customers, retaining the boxes herself. The customer would have to bring the key and open the box to make any credit purchase; the woman would place pebbles, counters or other items in the box to represent the amount of each credit sale, and would remove the appropriate quantity when cash payments were received.

8. Ask participants to share their experiences of other business record systems used by illiterate people. If time allows, ask them to talk to some business people and to find out what recording 'systems', if any, they use to help them manage their businesses. Stress that the way to obtain such information from business people is not to ask them if they keep this or that record, but to ask them how they decide about credit sales, or re-ordering, or their own withdrawals. Some literate business people keep records as they have been taught, but do not use them to make these or any decisions. Suggest that they, and the participants, can learn a great deal from what illiterate people do. It is better not to keep any records than to keep them and not use them.

9. Go through any common errors which have been made in the Enterprise Experience accounts and ensure that all participants understand them. They should use the enterprise experience as an opportunity to 'test' the kinds of records which they may ask their clients to keep. Are the records really practical to keep and useful for micro-business owners in managing their businesses, or are they a meaningless exercise?

What do goods and services cost?

OBJECTIVE
To enable participants to estimate the cost of the goods and services produced by micro-enterprises, to assess the impact of sales volume on costs and to estimate the 'break-even' point of a micro-enterprise.

TIME
One to one and a half hours.

MATERIALS

It may be convenient to prepare OHP transparencies, flip-chart sheets or simple handouts in advance, with the simplified figures for the tomato-vending business which is used as an example. It is important that the figures should be available throughout the session, whether they remain on the board or are presented elsewhere.

NOTE: This material is designed for participants to whom the concepts of fixed and variable costs and break-even point are quite unfamiliar. If some participants have some knowledge of these topics, they should use the session as an opportunity to practise helping others to learn. If the material is too elementary for all the participants, the session may be abbreviated and combined with the following one, or more examples may be added, using figures from the businesses which participants surveyed on the second day.

SESSION GUIDE

1. Write up or display the following very simplified figures for the daily operations of a woman selling tomatoes in the market, or, if they are suitable, use similar figures which were obtained by participants during their studies of micro-businesses earlier in the course.

		$
Daily sales, 20kg at $1.50		30
Cost of tomatoes, 24kg at $1.50 (wastage, 4kg)		24
Difference		6
Expenses		
Transport per day	2	
Market fee per day	1	
Total expenses		3
Profit		3

Ask participants to calculate the cost of the tomatoes per kilo, and allow five minutes for this.

2. Ask for their answers. Get the following alternative figures, all of which are correct:

	$
Purchase price per kg	1
Cost of saleable tomatoes per kg	1
Cost per kg. including expenses	$1.35

Some participants may also have included the woman's wage. There are many ways of doing this, such as:

- Using an average figure for a daily wage such as $2.

- Using the so-called 'profit' of $3.

- Using a higher figure which justice might suggest was appropriate, such as $4 or more, leading to a loss for the day's operations.

3. Ask for discussion on the issue of wages. Participants should recognize that although daily wages of $2 or even $10 can be argued to be fundamentally unjust, they are nevertheless the amounts that poor people actually earn, and many people earn even less than $2 a day, since casual workers on farms or construction sites and elsewhere are often paid far below so-called legal minimum wages.

Ask participants what would be the effect on their clients' micro-enterprises if they were to include in their prices 'socially just' wages, or even the legal minimum wage. Clearly many of them would not sell anything at all, since their prices would be far too high, and instead of earning a good wage they would earn nothing at all.

Conduct a discussion as to how this injustice can be corrected. Some exploited independent workers have successfully combined to secure higher wages, and NGOs have played a vital role in these achievements. For most poor people, however, such as the examples given above, dramatic improvements of this kind are not possible. The task of the NGO worker must be to help them to earn as much as they can in the existing situation.

4. Ask participants to suggest what might be a reasonable wage for a tomato vendor. Clearly the figures will differ from one area and possibly one season to another, depending on the alternative earning opportunities that may exist for people with the same skills, or lack of skills, in each case.

List generally agreed figures, such as the following:

Tomato vendor, wage of $2 per day, total costs	
$29, 20 kg daily sales, cost per kg	$1.45

5. Ask participants what determines the total cost, apart from the cost of tomatoes, wastage and the wage. Lead them to the answer that the quantity of tomatoes sold is a vital factor. In order to demonstrate this, allow participants up to 10 minutes to calculate the cost of one kilo of tomatoes, if the sales are 10kg per day.

Some participants may make the mistake of simply dividing the total cost figure by the new quantity of items sold, while others will probably have realized that the cost of the materials used will change in proportion to the quantity sold, while other costs will remain the same.

6. Look for the correct answer as follows:

	$
Materials (10 kg + 2 kg wastage, at $1)	12
Cost per kg sold at 10 kg	1.20
Wages, transport and market fee, unchanged expenses, total $5, expenses per kg sold at 10 kg	.50
Total cost per kg	$1.70

7. Participants may point out that the tomato vendor's transport cost might be reduced because she transported fewer tomatoes. They may also suggest that the vendor might wish, and indeed deserve, to pay herself more money, or less, so that the costs would vary more than is assumed in the above calculations.

Ask for discussion on these points, and if it appears that participants did not understand the above calculations, ask them to re-calculate the costs, but using their assumptions as to which costs would vary according to the volume of business, and which would remain fixed.

8. Ask participants whether the costs which have been assumed to be fixed in these calculations would remain fixed whatever the volume of business. Clearly they would not. If sales increased by two or three times, it might be necessary for the vendor to employ someone else to help her. If sales dropped to a very low level she might be able to spare enough time to find other part-time jobs, thus reducing the wage cost.

9. Ask participants to suggest businesses most of whose costs remain unchanged even if the volume of business changes significantly. Look for examples such as a porter, a bus, or a training course such as this one, where costs remain much the same regardless of the number of loads, passengers, or trainees.

Ask for examples of businesses where the costs vary directly according to the volume of business: list examples such as vendors or traders with no fixed premises, whose only fixed cost is their own wage. Ensure that all participants understand the difference between fixed and variable costs, and how to calculate the cost of each item produced or sold.

10. Display again the original figures for the tomato vendor, but without the sales figure. Ask participants to imagine that this is an estimate of costs and selling prices for a proposed new micro-enterprise. If they were asked to advise on its feasibility, they would have to help the woman to work out what would be the minimum necessary level of sales to cover her costs and earn the wage which was earlier agreed to be reasonable.

Ask participants to calculate the number of kilos of tomatoes she would have to sell in order to cover the fixed costs, including wages of $2 per day. Some participants should realize that the minimum level of sales can be calculated by finding out how much each kilo of tomatoes 'contributes' to the fixed costs, that is, how much of the selling price is left after deducting the variable costs per kilogram. The level of sales at which the fixed costs will be covered can then be calculated by dividing this 'contribution' per unit sold into the total of the fixed costs.

Lead them through the calculation as follows, ensuring that everyone understands each stage:

		$
Selling price per kg		1.50
Variable cost per kg		1.20
'Contribution' per kg		.30
Total fixed costs including wage	$5	
$5 divided by 3		1.66 or about 17 kg per day

Explain that they have now calculated what is called the 'break-even point' for the tomato vendor, that is, the level of sales at which she makes no profit and no loss.

This figure provides a vital guide when someone is proposing to start a new micro-enterprise, and it is also useful when advising somebody whose business is losing money. If it appears possible to reach the break-even point, it may be worth continuing the business, but if not, it may be necessary to make fundamental changes or even to close the business down.

What do goods and services cost? Part 2

OBJECTIVE
To enable participants to apply the lessons of the previous session to more complex micro-enterprises, including the real-life enterprises which they visited earlier in the course.

TIME
One to one and a half hours.

MATERIALS

The figures used in the previous session should be kept ready for display on OHP slides, flip-chart sheets or the board in this session, together with the figures for the village shopkeeper which are used at the beginning of this session. You should also have the figures which participants presented on the fourth day in Sessions One and Two, describing the businesses they studied the previous day.

SESSION GUIDE

1. The example that was used in the previous session was of a business where there was only one product, so that it was easy to divide the total costs by the quantity sold to obtain the cost per item.

   Display the following simplified statement of the monthly results of a village shop which sells a variety of goods:

		$
Monthly sales		1200
Cost of goods sold		<u>1000</u>
Difference		200
Expenses		
Rent per month	50	
Wage per month	<u>50</u>	
Total expenses		<u>100</u>
Profit		100

Ask participants to calculate the total cost of two typical items. In the above example, these might be one kilo of rice which the shopkeeper buys in a 50 kg sacks for $50 a sack, and one packet of biscuits which he buys in cartons of 24 packets for $9.60 a carton.

   Stress that the total cost means the minimum price at which the shopkeeper must sell the items in order to cover all his costs. Participants must calculate the variable cost per kilo and per packet, and then calculate how much the shopkeeper must add to the variable cost of each item in order to make sure that it bears its proper share of the fixed costs.

2. Elicit the following answers:

		$
Rice		
Variable cost per kg		1.00
Total fixed costs per month	100	
Total variable costs per month	1000	
Fixed cost = 10¢ per $1 of variable cost, or ten per cent		
Ten per cent of variable cost per kg		0.10
Total cost of rice, $1 + 10¢		1.10
Biscuits		
Variable cost per packet		0.40
Ten per cent of variable cost		0.04
Total cost of one packet 40¢ + 4¢		0.44

Ensure that participants understand that when a business sells more than one product, the fixed costs must be allocated according to some standard which can be applied to all the products. In the above case of a shopkeeper, it was the variable cost of the product. Ask participants to suggest a suitable basis for allocating fixed costs for other businesses, such as a tailor or a carpenter making different items.

Ask for suggestions such as allocating fixed costs according to the hours taken to make a garment or a product, or the distance travelled by a taxi.

3. Refer back to the example used in the previous session. Ask participants to suggest how they would advise the tomato vendor if she was considering reducing the selling price of her tomatoes. If she thought that she could double her sales, to 40kg per day, by reducing the price to $1.30 per kg, should she do it? Work through the calculation as follows:

	$
Sales, 40kg at $1.30 per kg	52
Variable costs, at $1.20 per kg sold	48
Difference	4
Fixed costs unchanged	5
Loss	1

Clearly she would be worse off than before, even though her sales were doubled, because she would only make ten cents towards her fixed costs on every kg she sold, instead of the 30 cents she made when her price was $1.50 per kg.

What should she do if she thought that she could increase her sales to 30 kg per day by making a smaller price reduction, to $1.45 per kg? Ask participants to work through the calculation as before:

	$
Sales, 30kg at $1.45 per kg	43.50
Variable costs, at $1.20 per kg sold	36.00
Difference	7.50
Fixed costs unchanged	5.00
Profit	2.50

This shows that lower prices can lead to higher incomes, provided that sales increase sufficiently. Similarly, higher prices can lead to lower incomes, or to higher incomes, depending on the effect that the changed prices have on sales.

Nobody can predict exactly how sales will be affected by price changes, but these examples show that it is quite easy to calculate what the effect of a given change in sales or prices will have on income. This method of calculation can help the owners of micro-enterprises, or those whose task it is to advise them, to assess the impact of possible changes and thus to make better decisions.

4. Refer to participants' enterprise experience businesses, which should by this time be familiar to everyone. Ask participants to identify those businesses which have a high proportion of fixed costs, such as an evening entertainment or weekend transport business, and those which have a high proportion of variable costs, such as a trading business where the owner only buys items which he is sure to be able to sell, or which he can return to the supplier if they are not sold.

Ask a volunteer to identify the variable and the fixed costs of her business. Write these on the board, and ask participants to calculate the break-even point. Initiate discussion as to the advisability of reducing or increasing prices, or spending more on promotion, in order to increase the profits of the enterprise.

5. Remind participants of the businesses they studied in the field earlier in the course. Choose one business for which the participants obtained reasonably complete figures for sales and costs, and write a simple summary of the operating statement of this business on the board, in the same form as the figures for the tomato vendor and the village shop. Ask participants to answer questions about this business such as:

- Which costs of the business vary according to the level of sales, and which are fixed?

- What is the total cost, including variable and fixed costs, of one typical item which the business sells?

- What is the break-even point of this business?

- If the owner was to reduce his prices by say one-tenth, by how much would his sales have to increase for him to maintain the same level of profits (or losses) that he is now achieving?

- If the owner was to increase his prices by a similar amount, by how much would sales have to fall in order for the business to reach the same level of profits as before?

6. Stress that techniques such as those which have been covered in the last two sessions are only of any value of they are *used* to help people to earn more money from their micro-enterprises. The ultimate objective should be to enable our clients to use these techniques themselves, without our assistance, so that they can become genuinely independent.

Ask participants to suggest how they would help an illiterate owner of a micro-enterprise, such as one of the people whose businesses they studied, or the tomato vendor, to understand the importance of distinguishing between variable and fixed costs, or to calculate the break-even point for her business. If time allows, set up a brief role-play. Ask one participant to act as the illiterate woman who proposes to start selling tomatoes, and another to try to advise her by helping her to assess the viability of her business by estimating costs and calculating the levels of sales necessary to make the business worthwhile, at various price levels.

Stress that it is often more difficult to explain even simple techniques of this sort to illiterate people than it is to understand them ourselves. Many illiterate people actually use these techniques already, although they do not use the written terms and calculations we use. Our task may be to learn from some of our clients, and to help others to share their insights.

Rates of return and the cost of money

OBJECTIVE   *To enable participants to assess the rate of return on capital of typical micro-enterprises, and to identify the significance of their findings to the setting of interest rates.*

TIME   *One and a half to two and a half hours.*

MATERIALS

The financial information which participants presented on the fourth day in Sessions One and Two, describing the businesses they studied the previous day, should be available for this session.

SESSION GUIDE

1. Remind participants of questions four and seven in the questionnaire which they filled in at the beginning of the course. Write up on the board the numbers of participants who thought that grants were better than loans, and who thought that the interest rate on loans should be below market rates of interest.

During this and subsequent sessions, participants will be examining the ways in which credit can be provided to poor people to help them start or expand micro-enterprises. Those whose NGOs are presently providing credit should be prepared to share their experiences, and those who are not will be able to learn from them, and from the experience of programmes elsewhere which will be discussed.

2. Ask each participant to think of a micro-enterprise with which she is familiar. This need not be the one she visited earlier in the course, since the objective is to gather information about a wide range of enterprises. It should, however, be a real micro-enterprise, established by a poor person and employing only its owner.

Allow five minutes for each participant to write down five facts about the business on a piece of paper:

- The type of enterprise it is.

- The total amount of capital invested in the enterprise.

- The average total earnings of the enterprise, including the owner's wage and the profit, if any, for a given period, such as a day or month.

- The amount the owner would have expected to earn in the same period, if (s)he had not been able to raise the capital to start her/his own business, and had instead to work for an employer. (Point out that this figure may be nil for some poor people for whom there are no employment opportunities of any sort.)

- The difference between the above amount and the earnings of the business.

115

Stress that the figures need only be rough guesses, since accurate information of this type is almost impossible to obtain.

3. Write the five headings on the board, leaving space for a further as yet untitled column on the right, and ask each participant in turn to read out what he has written and write the information in the appropriate columns. You may add the figures for the micro-enterprises which participants studied earlier in the course.

   You should then have a table in the following form, but with one set of figures for each participant. The figures in this example are those given by participants in a course in 1993.

Business	Capital	Earnings	Period	Alternative earnings	Difference
	$	$		$	$
Vendor	20	1	Daily	20¢	80¢
Village shop	100	20	Weekly	Nil	20
Barber	160	100	Monthly	60	40
Goats	300	100	3 Months	Nil	100

4. Now ask each participant roughly to calculate the percentage 'return on investment' for the enterprise he has described. That is, they should estimate the relationship between the additional earnings and the capital which has made it possible for these earnings to be made. Write in the figures, so that the table will now look like this:

Business	Capital	Earnings	Period	Alternative earnings	Difference	Percentage
	$	$		$	$	
Vendor	20	1	Daily	20¢	80¢	4%
Village Shop	100	20	Weekly	Nil	20	20%
Barber	160	100	Monthly	60	40	25%
Goats	300	100	3 Months	Nil	100	33.3%

Ask participants to consider why these percentage figures are important when we are discussing interest rates. Lead to the conclusion that the interest rate is what people *pay* for the money they borrow to finance micro-enterprises, and these percentage figures are what they *earn* with the money. One way of assessing what interest rate people can pay for money is to find out what profit they are going to earn from it.

   If participants find it difficult to grasp this, point out that borrowing money is actually the same as renting it. If somebody pays a landlord a certain monthly rent for a building and then rents it out again in turn, his profit will be the difference between the rent he pays to the landlord and the rent he receives from his tenants.

116

5. Ask participants to compare their percentage figures with the rates of interest charged by banks or money-lenders. In the examples used above, the four per cent earned by the vendor is clearly well below the lowest bank rates, and the other figures are not far above bank interest rates, and are far below money-lender rates.

By this stage one or more participants should have realized that the percentage figures they have calculated are not comparable with interest rates charged by banks or money-lenders, since interest rates are normally quoted on an annual basis, and the figures they have calculated are most likely to be for far shorter periods, as in the example above.

Ask each participant to re-calculate the rate of return for the business she described on an annual basis, making an approximate estimate of the number of days, weeks or months the business owner works in a year. They need not concern themselves with the difference between simple or compound rates. Erase the earlier percentage figures and replace them with rounded annual figures, so that the table will now look like the one below.

Business	Capital	Earnings	Period	Alternative earnings	Difference	Percentage
	$	$		$	$	
Vendor	20	1	Daily	20¢	80¢	800%
Village shop	100	20	Weekly	Nil	20	800%
Barber	160	100	Monthly	60	40	250%
Goats	300	100	3 Months	Nil	100	100%

(In the above calculations, the vendor worked 200 days a year, the village shop-keeper worked 40 weeks a year, the barber worked 12 months a year and the goat owner completed three three-month purchase and sale cycles in the year.)

6. Ask participants again to compare these percentage figures with the rates of interest charged by banks or money-lenders. In the examples used even the lowest rate is 100 per cent per year, which is well over what any bank charges, and is more than many money-lenders charge. These figures clearly suggest that poor people's micro-enterprises earn very high rates of return on the small amounts of capital they need to invest in them.

Stress that although these rates of return are far above what any large-scale entrepreneur or investor could ever hope to earn on his investments, this does not mean that the poor people are in fact rich. The actual amounts of money they earn are very small indeed, but because the investments in their micro-businesses are so small, the rates of return in percentage terms are very high.

Ask participants what this implies for interest rates. Clearly poor people can afford to pay what are apparently very high rates of interest for the small amounts of money they invest in their micro-enterprises.

7. Ask participants to work out the extra annual amount that a typical micro-enterprise will have to pay if the capital is borrowed at 30 per cent annual interest, rather than 15 per cent. Use a typical subsidized NGO or bank lending rate and the current open market rate for small loans rather than these figures, if possible. For the examples given above, the amounts will be as shown below.

	Capital $	Annual interest at 15% $	Annual Interest at 30% $	Difference $
Vendor	20	3	6	3
Village shop	100	15	30	15
Barber	160	24	48	24
Goats	300	45	90	45

The extra cost is significant, but it is not a large sum in relation to the annual earnings of the owner of the enterprise. It is unlikely to force the owner into destitution. Ask participants to write down what will be the effect on the lender, whether it is a banker or an NGO, if the interest rate is 30 per cent rather than 15 per cent per year.

8. Ask for their suggestions, and through appropriate questions try to list all the above effects on the lenders:

• They will make more profits, and will thus be encouraged to lend more.

• They will be able to pay more for their money, and will thus be able to attract more people to save money with them.

• They will be able to afford to employ more field-workers and to open more branches and provide better services to borrowers and savers.

• They will be able to reach out to more potential borrowers.

• More competitors will be encouraged to start lending, so that more and better services will be available to borrowers.

• The lenders will be able to absorb some losses if some people cannot repay.

9. Ask participants to write down what will be the effects of higher interest rates on the micro-enterprise borrowers, apart from the loss of a small proportion of their annual earnings, as already calculated. Establish the following effects:

• They will be encouraged to repay on time or early, because they will thus avoid paying more interest charges.

• They will be encouraged to save when they can afford it, and thus may not need to borrow next time they need finance.

• They will be encouraged to use their money productively and not to waste it, since they will have to earn a good return on it in order to pay the interest charges.

• They will be discouraged from borrowing more than they need.

• They will receive better services from the lenders, because they will be profitable customers rather than loss makers.

10. Ask participants to imagine themselves to be uneducated poor people who urgently need to start micro-enterprises in order to earn more income to feed and clothe their families. Write the following list of credit advantages for micro-enterprises on the board. Allow participants five minutes to rank them in order of importance, from one to five.

- Speedy decisions.

- Low interest rates.

- Informal, no forms to fill in.

- Located near to your home.

- No security required.

Ask them to read out and explain the ranking they have decided on. Summarize their conclusions on the board.

11. Ask participants to compare the services provided to poor people by money-lenders and by banks. Which comes closest to the rank order of features they have agreed on? Banks nearly always have the lowest interest rates, but they tend to be slow, formal, distant and to demand security. This is why money-lenders are still the main source of credit for the poorest people.

There are a number of ways in which NGOs can help the poorest people to obtain loans, at interest rates they can afford and with the other features which poor people need. In a later session participants will have the opportunity to observe and learn from one of the best-known examples.

The cost of NGO services

OBJECTIVE

To enable participants to appreciate the need to know the costs of the services they provide to their clients, and to calculate and to assess the consequences of these costs.

TIME

One and a half to two hours, or less if participants have been able to complete the exercise before the session.

ADVANCE PREPARATION AND MATERIALS

If time allows, distribute copies of the NGO costing exercise and ask participants to complete it before the session. NGO reports and accounts will also provide useful examples.

SESSION GUIDE

1. Ask participants briefly to name some of the services they provide for their clients. List a sample on the board, including activities such as training, extension, marketing, savings, credit and raw material supply. Do they know how much these services cost to provide?

Ask some participants who run training courses for their clients, or for their staff or others, to state the cost of one day of a typical training course for which they are responsible. Ask others who run credit programmes how much their programme costs, in terms of what it costs to lend and recover each dollar. Ask others still who are themselves field staff, or who are responsible for such staff, what one field-worker spending one day in the field costs.

Ensure that those participants who give a figure are actually including the overhead costs such as transport, management and premises, as well as actual staff salaries, and that they are taking account of the 'non-productive' days which most field-workers spend in the office, writing reports or attending internal meetings.

Some participants may know the costs of their own organization's services, while others may not, and others may not understand that they should. Ask participants to suggest why it is important that they should know them. List answers such as:

- NGOs, like any organization, must be able to evaluate their services by relating the costs of providing them to the benefits achieved. This is impossible without knowing the costs.

- NGOs should charge clients at least a small fee for most services. They must know their costs in order to be able to do this.

- Donors rightly demand to know what they are paying for. This is impossible unless the NGO knows its costs.

- NGOs have to plan and budget for their activities. They cannot do this unless they know what the activities cost.

2. If participants have already received and completed the exercise, ask one participant to suggest an answer to the first question, or distribute the exercise now, and allow participants up to half an hour to complete it.

The 'trick' of the first question is, of course, the omission of the number of people who will attend the course. Participants should quickly realize this, and ask for the number. Remind them of Day Six – Session Two, and ask them whether a tomato vendor knows how many kilos of tomatoes she will sell each day, or a taxi driver how many journeys he will make. Like the training institution in the exercise, they may know their maximum capacity, but that is all.

Training institutions have to base their prices on estimates like anyone else, unless they are fortunate enough to be able to persuade their customers to pay for complete courses, regardless of the numbers attending.

3. List the calculations as follows:

Fixed cost of the course:

		$
Staff salary: cost per day: 12 months at $1000 over 200 days	=	60
Overheads: cost per day: 12 months at $10 000 over 1000 days	=	120
Total fixed costs per day		180
Fixed costs of course, 5 days at $180		900
Variable cost per participant, 5 days at $5 per day		25

Cost each: for 30 participants: $30 + 25 = 55
for 20 participants: $45 + 25 = 70
for 10 participants: $90 + 25 = 115

As with any management problem, there is no right or wrong answer. The training institution should fix a price which appears likely to attract the number of participants they feel provides the best learning environment, and which is likely to cover the costs and earn some surplus. $75 might be a reasonable figure.

Stress the high proportion of fixed as opposed to variable costs which is normal for any service enterprise such as a taxi or a training organization. Ask participants what this implies for management. What is the best way of reducing costs and thus increasing efficiency for a training institution or any other NGO?

- Increasing the number of people who benefit from each course or other service, so long as this does not reduce the quality.

- Increasing the efficient use of all resources, including staff and physical facilities such as classrooms, vehicles and any equipment. People and facilities have to work harder!

4. Ask participants for their answers to the second question. This requires more calculations, and provides a useful exercise in simple arithmetic. Some, if not all, participants are sure to have made mistakes. Stress that none of the mathematics is beyond class five standard, and that it is vital that people who work in enterprise development work should be able to make correct calculations.

Some participants may be confused by the large numbers, and may put the decimal points in the wrong place. Stress that mistakes are not caused by ignorance but by carelessness. Remind participants of the session on quality, which applies to calculations as well as to products.

Stress that this exercise involves calculating the cost, and thus the selling price, or interest, to be charged for money, which is the 'product' that banks and NGOs which lend money are providing. As with tomatoes, training courses or rickshaw rides, the fixed and variable costs have to be identified and calculated. Elicit calculations as follows:

		$
Variable costs:		
Interest on the money to be borrowed from the scheme, 8% of $200 000		16 000
Write-offs @ 5% of 200 000		10 000
(The cost of interest written off has been omitted because it is a small amount and the calculation is complicated.)		
Total variable costs		26 000
Fixed costs:		
Office costs, 12 months @ $1000	12 000	
Transport costs	1000	
Training costs	5000	
Total fixed costs		18 000
Total costs		44 000
Amount to be lent		200 000
Interest cost, $44 000 on $200 000		22%

Some participants may think that 22 per cent is too high. Ask them how it might be reduced. Remind them of the example of the tomato vendor in the previous session, and lead them to the suggestion that as with any other product where the fixed costs are a high proportion of the total the best way to reduce costs is usually to increase volume.

5. Ask participants to suggest what might be the effect on the cost of the money if the NGO allows the groups to borrow $200 rather than $1000 each; elicit the following revised calculations:

		$
Variable costs:		
Interest on double the amount of money to be borrowed, 8% of $400 000		32 000
Write-offs @ 5% of 400 000		20 000
Total variable costs		52 000
Total fixed costs, as before		18 000
Total costs		70 000
Amount to be lent		400 000
Interest cost, $70 000 on $400 000		17.5%

This is still high, but is significantly lower than 22 per cent. Further reductions might be offered by the NGO, conditional on the rate of defaults being lower than the five per cent which has been allowed. Remind participants of the rates of return earned by micro-enterprises. They can usually afford to pay annual interest charges of 17.5 per cent or 22 per cent without difficulty, and the NGO might provide a more suitable 'marketing mix' for its clients by improving its services, and thus probably increasing its costs. As we saw in the earlier session, low interest cost is not necessarily more important to small borrowers than convenient, rapid service.

6. Ask participants to identify the variable costs of their own NGOs. They are likely to be very low in proportion to the fixed costs, unless they are involved in marketing or raw material supply. Stress again that every cost has to be controlled and kept as low as possible, but it is often better to increase the volume of services being provided, even if this means that some fixed costs have to be increased. 'Economies of scale' apply not only to manufacturing industries but also to NGOs.

DAY SEVEN — SESSION TWO

NGO costs, some exercises

Costing a training course

A training institution wishes to set the fee per participant for a new five-day course. Details of its current costs are as follows:

- Five teaching staff members are employed, at a salary of $1000 per month each. No other trainers are used, and the course will employ one of the teachers for the full five days. The classrooms can seat a maximum of 30 trainees.

- Each staff member teaches on average 200 days per year, so that the institution offers a total of 1000 days of teaching per year. It has no other revenue-earning activity.

- The total overheads of the institution in addition to teaching staff salaries are $10 000 per month, and the cost of files, handouts and other consumable items is $5 per trainee per day

- The courses are not residential, and trainees use their own money to buy their meals from neighbouring restaurants.

What fee per participant should they set?

Setting interest rates

An NGO wishes to borrow money from a new scheme in order to offer loans so the savings and credit self-help groups which have come up in the villages it serves can have access to more capital for lending to their members.

The groups have saved an average of $1500 each from their own money, and they are all very anxious to borrow more since many members have been unable to borrow enough for their needs. The NGO management have decided, however, that they will allow the 200 groups each to borrow only $1000 from the NGO, and the scheme will involve the following costs:

Interest to be paid on the loan made to the NGO	8% per year
Office and administration costs per month	$1000
Transport costs per year	$1000
Probable write-offs for unavoidable reasons	5% per year
Training cost for the groups per year	$5000

What rate of interest will the NGO have to charge to the groups in order to cover the costs of the scheme?

Marketing for NGOs

OBJECTIVE

To enable participants to apply the approaches and techniques of marketing to the relationships between their own NGOs and their clients and their supporting institutions.

TIME

One and a half to two hours.

ADVANCE PREPARATION AND MATERIALS

If possible, copies of the two case-studies should be distributed in advance of this session, so that participants can read them. You should also ask participants to bring examples of any promotional material from their organizations, such as reports or posters, whether this is directed at clients or at donors.

SESSION GUIDE

1. Remind participants of the 'four Ps' which they learned about in the earlier session. Some NGOs market raw materials to their clients, or clients' products such as handicrafts to other customers, but this session is concerned with how NGOs market their intangible services to their clients, and to donors.

Ask participants to list who their 'customers' are. Stress that every organization has to serve certain people, and they should be regarded as customers, or clients, even if they do not pay the full cost or even any part of the cost of what is provided. The first answer should be that an NGO's customers are the people whom it serves. If the NGO does not serve them properly, it will be failing in its task just like a commercial business which fails to satisfy its customers.

Ask participants to suggest why it is usually more difficult for an NGO, or any organization such as a government department, which does not make a full charge for its services, than it is for a commercial business, to be sure that it is serving its clients correctly. The response should be that the clients of competitive commercial businesses are free to buy their services from other suppliers if they are not satisfied, and the business therefore receives rapid 'feedback' from its clients. Their decision not to buy provides vital and immediate feedback and evaluation to the supplier. The clients of an NGO do not usually have the same freedom to move to another supplier, and the NGO, like a government organization, thus has a special responsibility to be sure that it is serving its customers correctly.

Ask participants to identify another quite different customer which NGOs have to satisfy, unless they are in the unusual position of having their own sources of funds. Elicit the answer that they have to satisfy the donors who support their work. NGOs have to market their services to both groups of clients, if they are to survive, continue and grow.

2. Divide participants into small groups. Distribute copies of the handouts if this has not already been done, and allow participants 15 minutes to read the case-studies.

Then allow the groups a further 45 minutes to agree on their answers to the assignments given at the end of both case-studies.

3. Reconvene the class, and ask one of the small groups what mistakes the manager of the ABC NGO made. Ask the other small groups to give their own suggestions, omitting any repetition, and list answers such as the following:

- He decided himself what training was needed. He did not try to find out what their real needs were, and if they really needed any training at all.

- The training was organized on a full-time basis, so that genuine full-time business owners would not be able to attend without damaging their businesses. The manager did not think about his clients' needs.

- The course was promoted in the newspapers and on television. The manager himself probably saw these regularly, but he did not put himself in his clients' position and ask himself whether they often read newspapers or looked at television.

- The course was free of charge, and included a stipend. This would tend to encourage 'free-loaders' rather than serious business people.

4. Ask another group to suggest how the manager of the ABC NGO should have marketed the course. Courage suggestions such as the following:

- The field-workers of the NGO should have told the local village people about the course during their work.

- The NGO should have asked local leaders, extension workers and others who worked in the villages to tell business people about the training.

- The training should have addressed the needs of the business people, and it should have been held in a village, probably in the evenings or at weekends.

- A small fee should have been charged to make the point that the course was worth attending and to discourage people who were not really interested.

5. Ask another group to say what mistakes were made by the director of the XYZ NGO. Ask the other groups for their views, and list answers such as the following:

- The donors were sent large quantities of general descriptive material, with no specific request for a particular amount of money to fund a specific project.

- The material was lengthy, and included no pictures or other supporting illustrations.

- The mailing bypassed the donors' local offices.

- The director ignored local donors, and did not try to build on the supporters the NGO already had.

- When the visitors came, they were given the impression that the NGO was very wealthy, and that its director had no genuine field contacts.

6. Ask another group how the director should have marketed her NGO to potential donors. Elicit suggestions such as the following:

- She should have started with the existing donors, and asked them for further contacts.

- She should have identified a small number of local donors, or local offices of foreign donors, and should have sent them short tailor-made letters, addressing their particular interests and inviting their representatives to visit the area.

- She should have taken their representatives to the villages, and showed them the day-to-day work of the NGO.

7. Ask participants to describe successful experiences of NGO marketing to their clients and to donors. Ensure that these are related to the 'marketing mix', and that participants appreciate that the basic principles of marketing are the same, whatever the product or service, and whatever the motives of the organization that is doing it.

Commercial businesses go bankrupt if they fail to market their products successfully, because their competitors take over their customers. NGOs are also operating in a competitive market-place.

Ask participants who their competitors are. Are other organizations trying to serve the same clients? Government agencies, banks and private firms are often involved in the same areas, and increasing numbers of NGOs are working in the field of enterprise development. In the long term, only those organizations which serve their clients cost-effectively, and market themselves successfully to those who pay for them, will survive.

The village enterprise training course

The training director of the ABC NGO was expecting a large number of suitable applicants for the new course on management for village enterprises which he had organized. He had made a special effort to design the course very carefully, and to inform people about it.

The course was designed for village people who had no formal business experience but were already in business and might wish to expand their enterprises. It was hoped that many women would come forward, since many of them were self-employed and it was felt that many of their businesses could successfully be expanded. The training director had spoken to a small number of such people. Most of them had little or no education, and it was clear to him that they needed to learn how to keep proper accounts for their businesses. This was to be the main topic of the course.

The course was planned to run for ten days full time, and the training manager had reserved a prestigious training centre in the city for the purpose. He had advertised the course in the local newspaper, and had successfully persuaded the television station to mention it in their local news bulletin.

He had hoped that people from all over the district would apply. There was no fee, since the expected applicants were very needy, and the NGO was offering free transport to and from the training centre, full accommodation and meals, and a small allowance to cover participants' personal expenses.

The training manager was therefore very disappointed when none of the applications he received were from the kind of people for whom the programme was intended. All the applicants were men, none of them was self-employed, and most were educated but unemployed young people from the city itself. None were from the rural villages as he had expected.

ASSIGNMENT

What mistakes did the training manager make in marketing his course, and what should he have done to recruit the kind of applicants he wanted?

The ambitious fund-raising campaign

The director of the XYZ NGO was determined to deal with the problem of shortage of funds once and for all. Her organization was engaged in a wide range of development activities in a very poor district, but it had for several years been forced to work on a hand-to-mouth basis, because although its work was locally recognized as being both effective and efficient, no regular source of support had been identified. The NGO had to rely on the goodwill of its voluntary workers and occasional donations from some wealthy local people.

The director wrote a forty-page description of the area where the NGO worked, describing the very bad conditions in which people lived, and including a general description of the NGO's work. She wrote a long letter appealing to people's spirit of charity and goodwill, and sent carbon copies of the letter and the descriptive document to the headquarters of about 100 official and voluntary donor organizations in Europe, Japan and North America.

After a long period she received replies from ten organizations, all of which said that they regretted they could not help. Two others which had local offices near the district where the XYZ NGO operated wrote saying they would like to visit the area.

The director took great trouble to arrange special programmes for their staff when they came, including a special dinner and meetings with local dignitaries in the best hotel in the city. She avoided any meetings with local supporters, since she wanted to be sure that the donors would think that her NGO had no other sources of money. A dancing group from one of the villages also performed for them, and the director made sure that the visitors did not have to suffer the discomfort of visiting the primitive rural villages.

After a long interval both of these NGOs also replied, thanking the director for her hospitality but regretting that they were not able to help. The director concluded bitterly that donors were not really interested in helping genuine organizations such as her own. She realized that she would now have to curtail her organisation's activities very substantially because of the shortage of funds.

ASSIGNMENT

What mistakes did the director make in marketing her NGO's work, and what should she have done?

Self-help groups and the marketing of credit

OBJECTIVE

To enable participants to identify the potential of self-help groups as a marketing channel for financial services, and to apply what they have learned about marketing to the provision of credit.

TIME

One and a half to two hours, depending on whether participants have read the case study before the session.

MATERIALS

Case study, the World's End Women's Group.

ADVANCE PREPARATION

The case-study should if possible be distributed well before the session, and participants should be asked on their own to complete the first part of the assignment.

SESSION GUIDE

1. Remind participants about the 'marketing mix'. Every organization has to design a suitable mix for its product and its customers. If its customers are poor people, particularly those living in remote areas or relatively inaccessible urban settlements, the choice of the right 'place', or 'distribution channel', becomes particularly important.

Ask participants to name the service which micro-businesses need most, and which governments and NGOs, as well as some banks, have tried with mixed success to market to them for many years through a range of programmes. Participants will of course be aware that this refers to credit. Stress that poor people, like participants themselves, need to be able to save as well as to borrow. They need full financial services.

One of the main problems in delivering such services has been the lack of effective 'marketing channels'. This means not only physical facilities such as bank branches, but also the people who provide the service. In most poor communities, money-lenders and traders still have a large share of the 'market'. They are successfully satisfying the 'place', the 'promotion' and the 'product' needs of their customers, and they are able to charge a high 'price' because there is no effective alternative.

The case study describes a new type of marketing channel which banks and NGOs have recently discovered can be a very effective way of marketing financial services: this is the self-help group. Groups of this sort exist in most villages. They may have evolved on their own or they may like the one in the case study have been suggested by NGOs. Most participants will be familiar with such groups, and some may already be working through them to provide financial services.

Very few NGOs are in a position to start a bank, since they are usually involved in a whole range of services in addition to savings and credit. This session and the next one are designed to help participants decide how their NGOs can most effectively market financial services through such pre-existing groups.

2. Divide the participants into small groups and allow 30 minutes to share the conclusions they came to individually on the first part of the assignment, and to prepare a brief presentation of their findings. Most NGO staff prefer to suggest what their clients should do, rather than genuinely empowering them by helping them to identify the options from which they themselves can choose. Stress that identifying the decisions which have to be made is often more difficult, and more important, than making the decisions themselves once they have been identified.

3. Reconvene the group, and ask a spokesperson from each sub-group briefly to list the options they have identified, in the form of questions which the group has to answer. Ensure that they focus on the decisions, or questions, and not on the answers. List their findings on the board, and ask each sub-group in turn to make its presentation, omitting decisions that have already been identified. The following questions should be identified. Encourage, through further probing those questions which groups themselves have not identified.

a. Should the group engage in lending activities at all, or should they not continue saving in order to accumulate more money in case of future personal or community emergencies?

b. If they do decide to invest their money in something other than a savings or deposit account with a bank, should they invest in a group activity such as the poultry farm or grain trading which some members have suggested, or should individual members borrow smaller sums of money for their own ventures?

c. Should the money be used only for productive enterprises or should it also be used for 'consumption' purposes such as buying food or medicine?

d. If individuals are to borrow the money, how should the group decide who should borrow, and in what order?

e. Should the group charge interest to its members on loans they take out?

f. If they do charge interest, what should the rate be and should it be uniform for all loans or varied depending on the purpose of the loan?

g. How should individual loans be repaid? Should the repayment schedule be flexible or fixed at the time the loan is taken, and should the rate of repayment be the same for all loans, regardless of their purpose?

h. How should the group deal with members who fail to repay on time?

i. If the group charges interest, should the 'profit' be distributed to members in some way, or should it be retained in the group fund for further lending?

j. Should the group consider some form of division into smaller sub-groups for day-to-day management?

Participants may mention many other issues. Ensure that there is no repetition, and that the focus is on fundamental rather than trivial questions.

4. Stress that there are many examples of successful groups which have answered these questions in different ways. Experience suggests that the important thing is to have made a clear decision which every member understands.

If time allows, briefly go through the questions and cite the arguments for each point of view. Stress again that there are no 'rights' and 'wrongs' in any of these issues. The task of an NGO worker is to help the group members themselves to identify and understand each issue and that they should participate in making a clear decision on each one. If participants have no opinions on any particular issues, it may be useful to stimulate discussion by mentioning some of the following points:

a. To invest or not? The group has already had an unsatisfactory experience with lending money from their fund, and it might be advisable to delay any use of the money until and unless the group is mature enough to be able to manage the complexities of investing. It is much easier and safer merely to save and deposit the money, and this alone provides the 'glue' which holds the group together for other purposes.

   The NGO should certainly not press the group to invest the money if they are at all reluctant. It is their money, and they should do with it as they will.

b. Group or individual enterprises? Experience everywhere with group enterprises has been bad. Grameen Bank in Bangladesh, which will be discussed in the next session, has moved away from this towards individual enterprises. Only a very strong group, with a very viable business idea, is likely to be able to overcome all the problems which are inherent in group management, and which we observed in the earlier session on this topic.

c. Production or consumption? This distinction is generally a false one, in that food and medicine are often very productive in the short term, since they enable people to work and earn money, and education is perhaps the most productive investment of all, although the returns may be delayed. So long as they can satisfy the group that they can repay, members should be able to borrow for whatever purpose they wish.

d. Who should borrow, and in what sequence? Members can draw lots, or they may agree on priorities through discussion, but it is important that everyone should have an opportunity to borrow before anyone borrows twice. The amounts and the repayment schedules should be designed to ensure that everyone gets a chance to borrow within say one year or 18 months. The office holders should be the last to borrow.

e. Interest or not? If the group fund is to maintain its value in spite of inflation, or is to expand at all, members must pay interest. Their payments will not be going to a money-lender or to a bank, but to their own fund.

f. What rate of interest? NGOs are usually all too aware of the extortionate rates charged by money-lenders, and may suggest a very low rate. Group members themselves, everywhere, usually prefer to charge themselves a very high rate, up to five per cent a month or more, because they understand the high rates of return they can earn from their micro-enterprises, as we saw in the earlier session. They should not be discouraged from this. It is usually advisable to charge the same rate for all loans, in order to make it simple and to avoid disagreements.

g. What repayment schedule? As with interest rates, it is easier and quicker to agree on one system of repayment, such as the Grameen Bank method of 50 equal weekly payments including interest, starting the week after the loan has been disbursed. This may not be easy for some agricultural investments such as the purchase of cattle or crop inputs which yield no return for some months, although many very poor people do manage to make regular repayments even before they earn any return.

h. How to deal with defaulters? Most groups achieve repayment records of well over 90 per cent, and even 100 per cent is common, because they can appraise and supervise their own enterprises far better than any outside banker or NGO field-worker. Every member knows that her own future loans depend on present loans being repaid. Some groups maintain a special emergency fund from a small proportion of all loans, or of interest payments, in order to cover members' unavoidable losses, and wilful defaulters should be very rare, because the group selects and controls its own membership.

i. Should 'profits' be distributed or retained? The interest payments are likely to be quite small for each member, and disagreements can easily arise over how they should be distributed. It is probably better to retain them in the group fund, in order to protect against inflation and expand the amount of money available.

j. Sub-groups? Most communities have found that groups of more than 15 people are unwieldy to manage, and it is better to have some form of sub-group division. This decision may be affected by issues of caste or gender, but experience world-wide suggests that smaller groups, of between five and ten people, are the most effective for day-to-day control of the routine of regular savings, credit and repayments.

5. Stress again that these decisions should be made in the context of each group's situation. If an NGO plans to make group-based savings and credit facilities available to large numbers of people, it will probably be necessary to standardize the rules and systems, but the above and other questions should be answered by each NGO after discussion with the people. Many NGOs have found that village people are already operating their own savings and credit systems, and have already answered many of these questions for themselves.

6. Ask participants to identify the fundamental limitations of credit of the type described in the case study. What prevents such group-based systems from expanding and providing larger sums, to more groups and thus to more people? Encourage the following suggestions:

- Not many NGOs have the management ability to assist such groups. This course is designed to help overcome this problem.

- The management ability and maturity of the groups themselves take time to evolve and develop. Excessive haste can be very destructive.

- Groups may be 'hijacked' by vested interests and pressure groups.

- The money available depends entirely on what the members themselves can save and reinvest. This will grow, but only slowly, while their problems are urgent.

Money may not be the main constraint, and too much money too quickly has often destroyed such groups. Nevertheless, many groups can make good use of additional money from other sources, such as NGOs or banks.

The next session will provide an opportunity to examine one well-known institution which uses client groups which have been set up according to its own procedures to bring financial services to some of the poorest people anywhere.

DAY SEVEN — SESSION FOUR; CASE-STUDY

The World's End Women's Group

World's End is a small settlement of thirty very poor families near the village of Poorland, some 15 kilometres from Cityville. In some seasons the men work on other villagers' farms, for around sixty cents a day, and at other times they walk to the city or to the neighbouring quarries, searching for casual work opportunities.

The women of World's End are generally badly treated by their husbands, who relieve the drudgery of their own lives by spending what money they have on traditional liquor. The women sometimes help their husbands in the fields, and some of them earn a few cents by selling firewood which they collect after taking their husbands' lunch out to them; few of their children go to school, they play around their huts, and when they are old enough they too get casual labouring jobs. Many girls of 12 or 13 years work in the quarries, carrying heavy stones on their heads. They are lucky if they earn more than thirty cents a day.

In 1984 a lady from Cityville started a voluntary society in Poorland. She first started a school for the girls from poor families, and she later recruited a number of like-minded colleagues, and some of the girls from the school also joined her as teachers and field-workers. She obtained funding from a number of sources, and the society started to offer a number of services, such as adult literacy training, basic health care and vocational training courses. The richer people in Poorland had at first resisted her efforts, but they soon recognised the quality of her society's services, and some even enrolled their children in the school, thus contributing to the breakdown of social barriers.

The field-worker who covered the area of World's End colony came to know some of the women there, and she suggested that they should meet together regularly to discuss their problems. She also suggested that they might start a group saving fund, since this was a useful way of maintaining a group's interest and commitment. After some discussion 28 women finally agreed to form a group, and they started regular meetings at the beginning of October 1991. They agreed to save ten cents a week each but even this involved some sacrifice for most of them. The women from the two poorest families in World's End were unable to join the new group, because they could not even put this sum aside, even though the other women offered to help them.

The group elected one of their number as President, who could write numbers and a few words, and whose husband was the only man in World's End with a regular job; they also elected a Secretary who could write her own name. All the other members were quite illiterate. At first many of the members' husbands tried to stop their wives from joining the group, particularly because they had agreed to hold their weekly meetings at 10 o'clock at night since this was the only time when they were free of other work, but the women felt for the first time in their lives that they were strong enough to resist this sort of pressure, and they successfully overcame the men's reluctance.

The field-worker had suggested that they should put their money in a savings bank account to keep it safe and earn some interest, but none of the members had any experience with banks. The field-worker had explained that the president and secretary would have to open the account in their own names, and be the only ones allowed to withdraw the money. Even so the other members feared that they might be tempted to steal their savings. They maintained a simple record of attendance at meetings and savings, and the secretary kept the money hidden in her hut. They also agreed to impose some discipline on themselves, and they fixed a fine of five rupees for non-attendance at meetings and five cents for late payment of weekly savings. These penalties were never actually imposed on anyone, but attendance and payments were always very regular.

The field-worker had maintained an interest in the group, and occasionally attended the meetings. In mid-1992 she suggested that the women might start borrowing from the fund, which had reached about a hundred dollars. After lengthy discussion they agreed to try; they settled on an interest charge of ten cents per dollar borrowed, regardless of the period and two members each borrowed $10 for grain trading; they repaid $11 dollars after two weeks. One of the Secretary's children then became seriously ill, and she urgently needed $10 for medicine. She repaid $12 after two weeks, because she was afraid that the other members would think she was exploiting her position of trust.

Although the three borrowers had each repaid promptly, a lot of ill will had been generated at the meeting when they discussed possible loans, so they decided not to allow any more borrowing. They kept on with their saving, however, and by February 1993 they had accumulated $205.60 plus some interest in their savings book at the nearest branch bank, which was on the outskirts of Cityville. The President's husband used to deposit the money for them regularly the day after every meeting, on his way to work.

At this point the field-worker suggested that they should think again about making some use of the money and at the next meeting some of them suggested that they might invest all the money in a joint activity; they might start a small poultry farm and sell eggs, since the money would be enough for almost a hundred birds and a simple shed, and or they could invest all the money in buying and selling grain. Most of the members wanted to take small individual loans for their own trading or other enterprises. They asked the field-worker what she thought they should do.

ASSIGNMENT

1. What are the main options facing the group? Identify them, do NOT suggest which choices they should make.
2. (AFTER identifying the options) Suggest what advice the field-worker should give about each decision.

The Grameen Bank, Bangladesh

OBJECTIVE

To enable participants to observe and learn from the experience of the Grameen Bank in Bangladesh, and to select from it those aspects which may be applicable in their own circumstances.

TIME

Twenty-five minutes video running time, preferably during the evening of the seventh day, followed by individual reading and group work. Preferably, a one and a half to two hour report-back session should take place the following day.

MATERIALS

Copies of the video, 'The Grameen Bank — A Bank for the People', and up-to-date information about Grameen Bank, can be obtained from Grameen Bank, Mirpur 2, Dhaka 1000, Bangladesh. The approximate cost of the video is $50. If these are unobtainable, you should use the case study without modification, and allow participants to read and discuss this without the video.

Test the video before the session as the English soundtrack may be difficult to understand. If so, listen to it carefully several times and prepare a rough 'script' in whatever language is most familiar to participants. Play the video to participants without the sound, and replace it with your own spoken commentary.

SESSION GUIDE

1. Tell participants that they are about to see and read about (or only read if the video is not available) a bank which has been set up in Bangladesh specifically to provide financial services to the poor. As they see or read about it, they should make notes in preparation for the group assignment, which is as follows:

- Identify the factors which have been particularly important for the success of the Grameen Bank.

- Identify policies and practices of the Grameen Bank which might usefully be applied in their own situations.

Show the video, and then distribute the case study. Divide participants into groups of not more than five people, and ask them to proceed with the assignment. If time allows, ask participants if they want to see the video again after reading the case study. If the video has been shown, point out that the figures in the case study are for 1993, eight years after the video was made.

2. Allow at least 30 minutes for small group discussion, after participants have seen the video and read the case study. Reconvene the class, preferably the next morning, and ask a member of each group to present her group's list of critical success factors.

List their findings on the board. They should include the following:

- Grameen Bank (GB) is a bank, not a 'project'. It is run like a business.

- GB concentrates on financial services. It does one thing, and does it well.

- GB was started by a local person, not by donors, and the initiative and control has remained local throughout. GB uses donors as a source of low-cost money, but it is not used by them.

- GB started as a small experiment, and its methods have evolved with experience. It was not a 'replication' which was imposed 'ready-made'.

- GB goes to the people, they do not even have to travel the two or three kilometres to visit their branches, except when their loans are disbursed.

- GB uses group pressure to ensure repayment, not physical collateral which poor people do not have.

- GB is not owned or controlled by government, but by its own members.

- The members have to learn the savings habit before they can borrow, and they have to continue saving.

- Strict discipline is imposed on all staff and on members, by themselves.

- GB is a new specialized institution, and has developed its own 'organizational culture' and trained its own staff.

- Staff are trained in the field, so that they and GB can be sure they are willing and able to do the work before they start their jobs.

- Successful staff are rewarded for their success, and if staff do not perform as required they can eventually be dismissed.

- GB is 'lean'. Staff travel by bicycle; they are paid at government rates; offices are very modest.

- Financial results are prepared and disseminated in a way that everyone can understand. They are ready in full less than a month after the end of the period to which they relate.

- Women make up the majority of the membership.

- Every loan has to be repaid within one year with regular weekly repayments.

- The maximum loan is so small that it is of no interest to richer people, and the interest rate is higher than for ordinary commercial loans, so that GB has not been hijacked by vested interests.

- Members pay for the emergency fund to insure themselves and their fellow group members. This avoids wilful default.

- The members themselves decide how they will invest their loans, there are no pre-prepared 'schemes' or preferential rates for particular types of enterprise.

- Loans are appraised by the members of the borrower's group, who know what their fellow villagers can and cannot do far better than any outsider ever could.

- Borrowers' use of funds is monitored by their fellow members, not by paid bank staff.

3. Participants should not regard GB as perfect. Ask if any of them have any adverse comments. If so, ask them to state them, and if not, list these and other points of view, with contrary arguments such as are suggested, and encourage some discussion:

- Saluting and drill are more suitable for armies than for a bank. This is a common comment, but GB uses these techniques not for military purposes, that is to kill people, but to create the sense of discipline that is needed to achieve the high rate of repayment.

- GB offers nothing to members who need larger loans in order to 'graduate' to larger enterprises. GB helps millions of poor people to become less poor. Their systems are designed to do this, and they would be weakened if they tried to do different things.

- Members become permanently indebted to GB, they can never become independent. Many, if not most, richer people are in debt for much of their lives: through bank overdrafts, hire purchase debts, credit societies and other means. GB extends the same facility to the poor.

- GB depends on the 'charisma' of its founder, Professor Yunus. This was certainly true at the beginning, but as GB has grown powers have been delegated and Professor Yunus now spends very little time on day-to-day management.

4. It is important not to give the impression that GB, or any other system, is a 'model' which can be applied ready-made in another environment. Ask participants to suggest particular features of the environment in which GB operates which are different from their own. These may include:

- The rural population in Bangladesh is very concentrated, so that large numbers of people and many villages can be reached from a single branch.

- There are, generally speaking, few communal divisions in rural Bangladesh, so that the group mechanism can be more effective.

- Banks are usually not able to charge interest rates on small loans at a level which would cover the cost of the services which GB provides. Even if they could, their management may be unwilling to allow the apparent injustice of charging poor borrowers high interest rates.

Participants may have other comments. These should be discussed, but it is also important not to allow participants to concentrate on the reasons why elements of the GB approach cannot be applied in their own situations. It is always easier to argue why things cannot be done than to find ways in which they can be done.

5. Ask participants to share the conclusions from their small groups as to which aspects of the GB system they themselves might apply in their own organizations. Stress that they need not and probably could not apply the whole system, but that

any NGO which is offering, or plans in the future to offer, credit can learn something from GB. Encourage suggestions such as:

- Introduce a prior savings requirement as a condition of eligibility for loans.

- Introduce regular weekly repayments.

- Use existing group structures which may have come together for other purposes as a delivery mechanism for financial services.

- Delegate loan appraisal to groups of borrowers themselves.

- Make the financial services component of an NGO into a discrete self-accounting entity, with separate management and the eventual intention of it becoming a financial institution.

DAY SEVEN — EVENING SESSION and

DAY EIGHT — SESSION ONE; CASE STUDY

The Grameen Bank, Bangladesh

The Grameen Bank was established in 1976 by Professor Mohammed Yunus. He saw how difficult it was for landless village people to earn enough to live on, because they could not even afford the tiny amounts of capital needed to undertake local economic activities. The money-lenders' interest rates were so high that they absorbed most of whatever people could earn.

He started by lending a small sum from his own money to a small group of women, and when they paid it back exactly as agreed he eventually managed to persuade the local commercial bank to lend him money for more loans of this type. They said that they could not lend directly to uneducated village women, who had no collateral, could not possibly cope with the formalities of borrowing and would certainly not be able to repay. Professor Yunus was convinced that the conventional bankers were wrong, and he extended his own experiments. In spite of his efforts to work with the existing commercial banks, it eventually became necessary to set up a completely new bank, and the Grameen Bank was incorporated in 1983.

The system, which has evolved over time and is indeed still developing, is based on 'groups' of five members, which are organized and brought together in 'centres' of about seven groups. Only the very poorest people are eligible for membership, and the bank workers visit every prospective member's home to ensure that they do not have more than $400 of assets or half an acre of land. Traditional bankers are astonished at a bank which insists that its borrowers should not have collateral, but they are also astonished by the average repayment rate of 98 per cent which the Grameen Bank achieves.

The group members have to learn the simple procedures of the bank, and to sign their names, but they do not receive any training in business or in the activities they wish to undertake. After they have demonstrated their solidarity by meeting promptly at a fixed time and saving a small sum regularly every week for a short period, they become eligible for loans. They also have to learn some simple physical exercises and a drill which they go through at every meeting.

The members themselves decide what activities they will undertake, and how much money to borrow. The average loan is around $100, and the maximum is $300. The members know what activities are viable in their communities, and what their fellow villagers can do, and the bank has so far financed more than a thousand different types of activities.

The bank worker, who bicycles out to attend their weekly meeting in the village to collect their savings and repayments and to receive new loan applications, merely checks that the application is in order and that the whole group, and the centre, are in favour of it. This is vital, since every member of a group, and eventually a centre, is responsible for every other members' repayments in case of default, and no member of a group can apply for a new loan if any other member is in arrears.

Loan applications are approved and disbursed within ten days at most, and the only time that the members have to visit their branch is when their loans are disbursed. All their other banking business is transacted at the weekly meetings, which usually take place early in the morning before farm work begins. Discipline and punctuality are strongly enforced by the members themselves. If a member, or the bank worker, is even a few minutes late for a meeting, he or she pays a fine into the centre's fund.

Every loan has to be repaid in 50 weekly instalments, starting the week after it is disbursed. Interest is charged at 20 per cent per year, but when the total of the various savings and emergency insurance fund contributions that members have to pay is added to the interest the total actually amounts to over 30 per cent of the loan amount. This is well over the rate charged by commercial banks but the members pay without difficulty and the high rate, as well as the small loans and regular repayment, ensure that only people who really need the money will try to join. Richer people can get larger loans more cheaply elsewhere.

The bank has grown rapidly. By December 1993 it had 1040 branches, working in 33 667 villages, and 1.8 million members, of whom 94 per cent were women. There are about 12 000 members of staff. They are paid at the same rates as government employees, and they are trained for six months, largely in the field. A number resign at this point, which ensures that only those who are committed to the bank's philosophy are finally employed. Monthly financial accounts for the whole bank, and for each branch, are produced and circulated within three weeks after the end of each month. The manager and staff of particularly successful branches receive substantial bonuses. Staff who fail to perform are warned and may eventually be dismissed.

In the early years the government contributed substantial capital and was the majority shareholder, but later on the bank's capital requirements exceeded the government's ability to subscribe. The members now own 95 per cent of the shares, through converting a part of their savings into share capital. Nine of the 12 directors are women members from villages, elected by their fellow members. Apart from the members' savings and equity, the bulk of the funds come from loans to the bank from overseas, which are generally made on concessional terms but do have to be repaid. Grameen Bank is a bank, not a project.

The following simplified set of the bank's accounts for 1993 shows the sources and uses of money, and the operating income and expenses. The amounts paid and received for interest on borrowing and loans work out at far less than the actual rates paid and charged, because the bank was growing so fast during the year.

Grameen Bank, Bangladesh
Summarized accounts for year ending 31 December 1993

Approximate balance sheet as at 31/12/93

Sources	$ Million	Uses	$ Million	
Capital	5	Cash	negligible	
Reinvested profits	1.3	Bank short-term accounts		11.2
Revolving fund	95	Bank fixed deposits		60
Borrowings	183	General loans	207	
Members' deposits	105	Collective loans	0.4	
Current liabilities	21	Housing loans	86	
Profit for year	0.3	Special project loans	4.5	
Total	410.6	Staff loans	1.5	
		Total loans	299.4	
		Less provisions	6.7	
		Net loans		292.7
		Interest receivable	31	
		Less provisions	1.8	
		Net interest receivable		29.2
		Buildings and equipment		17
		Other uses		.5
		Total		410.6

Profit-and-loss account for 12 months to 31/12/93

		$ Million
Income:	Interest on Loans	35.1
	Interest on investments	5.7
	Training grant	2.9
	Other income	0.4
	Total	44.1
Expenses:	Interest on deposits	5
	Interest on borrowings	7.9
	Salaries and allowances	19.3
	Depreciation	0.6
	Training costs	1.6
	Provisions	6
	Other expenses	3.4
	Total	43.8
Net Profit		0.3

During 1993 the Grameen Bank disbursed general and collective loans to a total value of about 350 million dollars, with a further 55 million dollars of housing loans. Recoveries remained at 98 per cent.

Micro-credit — who does what?

OBJECTIVE   *To enable participants to identify different approaches to the delivery of financial services to their clients, and to select an appropriate delivery system for their own NGO.*

TIME   *One and a half to two hours.*

SESSION GUIDE

1. Remind participants of the content of the previous two sessions, which dealt with different ways in which financial services can be marketed to clients. The Grameen Bank method requires a complete system, which is beyond the scope of most NGOs, although every NGO can learn from it. The World's End Women's Group case study described a group which is learning to run its own savings and credit facility, without involving any financial contribution from the NGO.

Groups of this sort can be very effective, but they depend entirely on what they themselves can save and reinvest. Ask participants why it is that NGOs may wish to provide such savings and credit groups with more money. Encourage answers such as:

- Poor people need more money than they can save, and more quickly, to start and expand their micro-enterprises and thus boost their incomes.

- Banks have traditionally taken savings deposits from the poor and lent the money to the rich. Only very few rural bank branches lend out even the same amount of money as they take in deposits, and many lend less than a half or even a fifth of their deposits. If poor people can have access to some of this money, which comes from their own communities, it will help redress the balance.

- Society in general has for many years exploited the rural poor by using their natural resources and their labour for little or no payment. Credit groups provide a means by which this exploitation can begin to be corrected.

- As we saw earlier in the course, the micro-enterprises of the poor earn far higher returns on the small amounts of money invested in them than larger businesses. Micro-enterprises are a profitable investment for their owners, for society in general and for anyone who lends money to be invested in them.

2. There is thus a clear case, in terms of both economics and social justice, for making more investment money available to the poor. One reason why so little capital has actually flowed to poor people, however, apart from the natural desire of the rich to maintain their position, is that it is not easy to deliver capital effectively to poor people.

Savings and credit groups can provide a remarkably effective delivery channel for capital, but there are many difficulties in the process of enabling purely self-financed groups such as the World's End Women's Group to gain access to

144

additional money from outside their own communities. Ask participants to identify some of these, and list the following:

- It is more difficult to manage larger sums of money, whatever their source. A group which can successfully manage its own credit fund, which only increases gradually from its members' savings and interest payments, will not necessarily be able to manage a larger amount of money, particularly if there is a sudden increase.

- When the members of a group know that the money in their fund is all the result of their own savings and reinvestment, they will value and take care of every rupee. If the money comes from some outside source, such as a bank or an NGO, they will not feel they 'own' it in the same way.

- When money comes from outside, it inevitably brings outside power and influence with it. This complicates the process of using the money, and may totally corrupt and destroy a group which was quite able to manage its own funds.

- Banks may be unwilling to lend to or even to take deposits from unregistered groups, and registration may involve costly and lengthy formalities and may even introduce political interference.

- In some communities a large proportion of the population may already be defaulters under other schemes, often because they were manipulated by others who expropriated much of the money. Banks may not be willing to lend money to a group even if only one member is a defaulter.

3. Some NGOs, and some banks, have successfully overcome these problems and have enabled client groups to access, use and repay outside funds. As with the management of the groups themselves which was dealt with in the earlier session, there are many ways of doing this. The choice will depend on the nature and situation of the various parties involved, including the members, the groups, the NGO and any others. What is important is that everyone should know what has to be done and who is responsible for doing it. This is, after all, what good management of any activity really means.

4. Ask participants to recall the group described in the World's End Women's Group case study. If the NGO in this case study had promoted several such groups, all of which had shown themselves capable of managing the process of saving, borrowing from and repaying their own funds, how might the NGO enable the groups to obtain more money to increase their funds more quickly than their own money would allow?

Elicit suggestions such as obtaining money from local or foreign donor organizations, or from a financial institution. Participants should imagine that they represent the NGO in the case-study. If they wished to enable the groups to get access to money from a bank or other financial institution, what alternative routes are there whereby the money might reach the groups, and thus their members?

List the four 'players' on the board, and ask participants to suggest different ways in which the money might flow to the members; illustrate these by appropriate lines and arrows, as below:

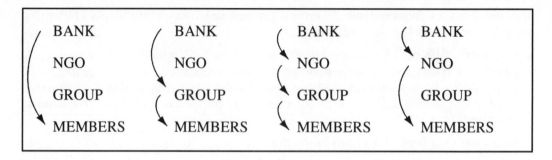

Ensure that participants identify the basic issue of responsibility for lending and borrowing:

- Should the NGO actually borrow from the bank, and re-lend to the group, or should the bank lend direct to the group, with the NGO acting as a facilitator, or possibly a guarantor, but not as an intermediary?

- Similarly, should the group borrow from the bank or the NGO, as the case may be, and re-lend to the members, as in the previous case-study, or should the members borrow from the bank or the NGO, as in the case with Grameen Bank, Bangladesh, with the group acting as a facilitator and/or guarantor?

Stress the importance of being clear as to the actual flow of money, and thus the responsibility of each party.

Each of the above approaches has been successfully adopted by NGOs in various countries. There are advantages and disadvantages to each of them. Discuss these, and ask participants to suggest which approach might be most suitable for their own organizations.

5. Some participants may come from NGOs which can obtain subsidized funds and grants from donors, and others may have their own resources. They may therefore feel that they have no need to try to gain access to money from banks.

Ask participants to suggest good reasons for avoiding the banks and trying to rely on their own resources, and encourage the following suggestions:

- Banks tend to be bureaucratic and slow. Poor people cannot cope with complicated formalities and they need money quickly.

- Bankers have come to regard poor people as high-risk borrowers, who cannot be considered as genuine customers who can make good use of capital and repay it, but only as objects of charity or recipients of loans which government forces the banks to provide.

- The people themselves have come to regard the banks as an arm of government, which provides them with subsidies and loans which need not be repaid.

There are, however, many reasons why NGOs should try to help their clients to obtain access to bank finance, in spite of the difficulties. List the following reasons for attempting to do this:

- Banks have extensive branch networks, which have facilities and staff for handling money. NGOs can never hope to rival these networks.

- Donor and NGO funds are limited, and only a small minority of poor people can be reached by those agencies which have access to such funds. The objective should be to make micro-credit as universally available as Colgate toothpaste, and this can only be done if the banks are involved.

- Donor and NGO funds necessarily involve dependence. If poor people can be put in a position to borrow money from banks they will thus be enabled to enter the mainstream of the economy.

- If bankers are introduced to groups as good customers, they will be encouraged to maintain and expand their business in poorer areas.

Some banks are also trying to develop groups themselves, without any assistance from NGOs. They are doing this not only because they have a sense of social responsibility, but because they recognize, like manufacturers of the consumer products which have already been mentioned, that they must reach out to the mass market if they are to expand their own banking businesses.

6. In addition to the actual tasks of lending and borrowing money, there are also a number of other functions which may have to be undertaken if groups are successfully to 'graduate' from using only their own money to accessing other funds. Ask participants to suggest what these may be, and name examples such as:

- Training the groups in how to manage their money.

- Keeping records of individual savings and of loans and repayments.

- Selecting the borrowers.

- Selecting and managing the enterprises.

- Pressing for recovery of loans.

- Guaranteeing repayment in case of default.

Draw a simple matrix on the board, with the 'players' across the top and a list of tasks such as the above down the side, and ask participants to suggest which tasks should be undertaken by which 'players'.

	Bank	NGO	Group	Member
Training		X		
Records			X	
Selection			X	X
Managing				X
Recovery			X	
Guarantee	X	or	X	

The above allocation represents only one point of view. Stress that as with the actual lending and borrowing, there are many different approaches. What is necessary is that everyone should know who is responsible for what.

7. Some participants may have extensive experience of working with client savings and credit groups, while others may not have entered this field at all. Stress that not every NGO should become involved in it, since it requires a very high standard of

management to be effective, but it is possibly the most effective single way of empowering poor people, since it puts resources into their hands, for them to use as they think fit in improving their position.

In many countries, it is possible to recognize a member of a successful savings and credit group because he (or more usually she) has the confidence to look strangers in the eye directly. This is a simple and dramatic visible sign of empowerment.

Self-sustainability for NGOs

OBJECTIVE

To enable participants to define self-sustainability in their own institutions, and if appropriate to plan towards achieving it.

TIME

One to one and a half hours.

SESSION GUIDE

1. Many NGOs advocate and attempt to practise 'participative development', but their own management is not participative at all. Junior staff feel that they have no role in policy decisions or the direction of the organization. This session should be used not only to develop ideas for sustainability, but also to begin to make participants, at whatever level, understand that everyone in an organization can and should be allowed and encouraged to contribute to its management.

Ask participants to write down, in a line or two at most, what they understand by the term 'self-sustainability'; how can one say that an NGO is, or is not, self-sustaining? Allow up to five minutes for this. Ensure that more senior-level staff do not dominate the session. Ask participants for their suggestions, and elicit, by further questions if necessary, a range of answers covering the complete spectrum from complete reliance on one donor to total cost recovery, including the cost of capital, from fees paid by clients for services rendered.

2. List their answers on the board, in order of 'rigour', in the following form:

- Total reliance on one donor for all income.

- Total reliance on a spread of donors.

- Part reliance on income earned from contracts from donor sources to provide services or run projects, as opposed to simple grants.

- Total reliance on income as above.

- Part reliance on own income from investments or profitable businesses owned and managed by the NGO.

- Total reliance on income as above.

- Partial reliance on fees paid by clients for services received.

- Total reliance on such fees, like any business.

There may be many quite different answers, but it is important for participants to understand that the term can be defined in many different ways, and that complete self-sustainability, in the most rigorous sense, actually means that an NGO becomes a business enterprise, and is not really an 'NGO' any more.

3. Ask participants to suggest how close their own NGOs are to real self-sustainability. Are they trying to move more in this direction, should they be, and why do most NGOs try to move further towards a more rigorous form of self-sustainability? Encourage suggestions such as:

- To respond to donor pressure for a measure of self-sustainability as a condition of future support.

- To avoid the risk of relying on one source of funds which might be withdrawn.

- To obtain greater autonomy through reduced dependence on external sources of support.

- To enhance clients' and the NGO's own staff self-respect by reduced reliance on charity or subsidy.

- To demonstrate their own success by developing their clients' ability to pay part and eventually the full cost of the services they need.

4. Ask participants to write down as many different ways as possible by which an NGO might attempt to increase its income, other than by seeking for donor funds. Encourage them to be wide-ranging and even 'wild' in their suggestions, since this form of 'brain storming' is often the most effective way of identifying innovative approaches to the solution of a problem.

Allow up to ten minutes for this, and then ask each participant in turn to make one suggestion. Go round the complete group, and then ask for second and subsequent suggestions until nobody has any more ideas. If necessary, elicit further ideas such as the following by appropriate questions. Stress that every one of the following methods of raising money is successfully being used by NGOs to reduce their dependence on donors, and there are no doubt large numbers of other possibilities.

- Provide consultancy for other NGOs, for a fee.

- Provide training for staff of other NGOs, for a fee.

- Charge market rates of interest on credit to clients.

- Charge clients a fee for training.

- Organize guided tours for foreign visitors.

- Charge fees for guest-house accommodation.

- Rent out office space.

- Raise a capital fund, and cover costs from interest earnings.

- Charge students for field research facilities.

- Make a charge for transport services.

- Sell videos of development activities.

- Buy and resell client handicrafts for a profit.

- Sell raw materials to clients at a profit.

- Raise funds from small donations from local people.

- Organize fund-raising events, sponsored walks and so on.

- Seek corporate sponsorship from large businesses operating in the area.
- Provide rural market research facilities for manufacturers.
- Charge visitors for the time they occupy.
- Sell photocopying and other office services.
- Sell computer training to other NGO staff.
- Sell computer software designed for NGO management.
- Rent out meeting-room facilities.

Some at least of their suggestions should be based on their own practical experience. Ask those who have made use of particular methods of fund raising briefly to describe their experiences.

5. Ask participants to suggest what problems their own organizations might face if they attempted to introduce such methods of raising money. Remind them that staff of NGOs which wish to promote enterprise must themselves be enterprising, and that entrepreneurs are people who see opportunities when other people see problems.

Ask the participants from each NGO which is represented on the course to identify at least one new opportunity for raising money which their NGO might use, and to make a rough estimate of how much money it would be possible to raise each year in this way. Allow up to 15 minutes to do this, and then ask them briefly to present what they propose to do.

Invite comments from other participants. There is always a tendency to suggest why new things cannot be done. Try to steer participants towards a more 'enterprising' attitude, so that they try to suggest ways in which their colleagues can indeed do what they have suggested, or can possibly even do much more. Stress that it is unlikely that any single innovation such as has been suggested can make an NGO self-sustaining. What is important is to establish a climate where every staff member is encouraged to look for ways to improve the independence and efficiency of the NGO by reducing costs and increasing revenues.

Remind participants that on the last day of the course they will have to present their 'action commitments', or statements of a particular change they are proposing to introduce on their return to their work. The ideas that they have just presented may have the potential to be developed into such commitments.

6. The next sessions will provide an opportunity for participants to assess the present and potential future position of their colleagues' NGOs, and to make recommendations for improvements, in the same way as they earlier assessed individual micro-enterprises.

Stress that every NGO should be looking for new ways of reducing its dependence on donors. Some of the ideas for raising income which have been suggested in this session should be useful in their recommendations for the future of their organizations.

Financial appraisal of NGOs

OBJECTIVE

To enable participants to apply to NGOs what they learned earlier in the course about rapid financial appraisal of micro-enterprises, in order to identify the critical factors and to recommend and assist in the implementation of change and improvement.

TIME

One and a half to two hours (if necessary, the session may be shortened by omitting one or even two of the three case studies. They need not be linked to one another).

ADVANCE PREPARATION AND MATERIALS

If possible you should prepare simplified accounts from the reports and accounts of their own NGOs which some participants should have brought with them, on the same model as the three sets of data which are provided at the end of the session. This simplification is not easy, and you may need someone with more expertise in accounts to assist, but it is vital that you yourself, as the instructor, should fully understand the process. If you cannot create new case-studies from participants' own NGOs' accounts, the 'ready-made' accounts and case-studies for NGOs numbers one to three may be used.

SESSION GUIDE

1. Ask participants to recall if they have ever come across situations such as the following in their own or in other NGOs:

- An NGO is required to submit audited accounts but has failed to maintain even the minimum records needed by an accountant.

- An NGO runs a loan scheme but does not have up-to-date and accurate records of exactly how much each client owes.

- An NGO cannot cover its central administration costs because grants only cover programme field costs.

- An NGO commits itself to expenditure which is not covered by expected income.

- An NGO uses money which has been donated for a specific purpose for a quite different purpose, such as covering headquarters' salaries.

Participants will probably know of these or similar problems. Allow a few minutes for them to describe examples of incidents of this kind.

2. Ask participants to relate these or similar problems to management failings of micro-enterprises. What errors or omissions are the managers of these NGOs

making, in terms of business management? Encourage suggestions such as the following, which relate to the examples given above in item 1:

- They are not keeping business records.

- They are not keeping up-to-date or accurate records of who owes what to the NGO. They do not have a good record of accounts receivable.

- They do not know the costs of their goods or services.

- They have failed to include overheads in their costs.

- They are not managing their cash flow properly.

- They are misusing money.

Why is it particularly important for NGOs which are working in enterprise development to avoid such management errors? Clearly, an NGO which does not keep a record of its own accounts receivable, or does not know its own costs, is not likely to be able to assist its clients to do these things for their micro-enterprises.

3. Ask participants to suggest important policy questions which often confront the management of NGOs. List examples such as:

- Should the NGO concentrate on one function, such as training, credit, or marketing, or should it try to offer a full range of services?

- Should the NGO try to expand or should it remain at the same level?

- If the NGO wishes to expand, should it do so by offering the same services to new clients, or by offering new services to its existing clients?

- How should the NGO deal with the departure of a charismatic leader who started it or brought it to its present position?

- How should the NGO diversify its sources of support?

- How can the NGO retain its sense of mission and commitment and at the same time become more businesslike and self-sustaining?

Stress that many NGOs, like other organizations, fail to achieve their objectives not because they answer such questions wrongly but because they never ask them at all. The most valuable service which outsiders, or staff members who have been away to training courses, can provide is often not to suggest the answers but to identify the questions.

Remind participants of the earlier session when they appraised real micro-enterprises in the field, and then reported on their findings and recommendations. They have also discussed marketing and costing for NGOs in earlier sessions. They will now apply to NGOs the simple tools of financial analysis which they used for appraising the enterprises which they visited earlier in the course.

The three simple case studies to be used in this session consist of simplified versions of balance sheets and profit-and-loss accounts for three real NGOs. The cases are disguised, but the figures are real. The cases focus on the financial information, not because other things are not important but because such information is so often neglected by NGOs and their advisers.

4. Distribute the accounts for NGO number one. Allow participants up to 15 minutes to study them on their own and to be ready to comment on the financial

management of the NGO and on any other issues which the accounts suggest. Stress that the main purpose of analysing accounts in this way may be to prompt questions. As we have seen before, asking the right questions is often more difficult than answering them.

Some participants may find the figures too large and too complicated. Stress that they have actually been substantially simplified. Most NGOs have several thousand dollars worth of assets and annual revenues, and their accounts have many more items than these examples. All staff members should be able to understand them, and to explain them to their colleagues who do not. Ask the group for their comments and questions. Issues raised should include the following:

- If the value of stocks is divided by the annual cost of goods ($27 000 over $133 500 = about one-fifth of a year or two and a half months), it shows that almost two and a half months of sales are held in stock. This is not excessive for handicrafts, but it may conceal some fast-moving items and other slow-moving or dead stocks.

- If the accounts receivable are divided by the sales ($44 400 divided by $152 500) it shows that the NGO is giving approximately three and a half months' credit. This is high, and is tying up money that could be used otherwise, but it may be because export customers or others are unable to pay more promptly.

- The costs of the NGO's dairy are almost double the sales of milk. This may be because much of the milk is consumed by the staff, or donated to needy people, but it may reveal a typical example of an 'income-generating enterprise' which in fact generates no income for the NGO and makes a loss. It should be investigated.

- The trading operation on its own is making an annual loss of $5000, which is covered by non-trading income. This is reasonable, considering that the producers need a high level of service, but in the interest of the artisans the NGO should help them understand and work towards standards of quality and prices which will enable them eventually to sell outside the 'sheltered' NGO and alternative trading market.

5. Deal with the accounts for NGO II in the same way. Explain that the 'capital fund' refers to the money used to set up the NGO, like the owner's capital for a business. The issues raised by participants should include the following:

- This NGO is not trading, like NGO I, and the majority of its expenses are covered by grants. About ten per cent of its income is coming from non-grant sources. This represents a beginning on the road towards self-sustainability.

- The equipment sale is probably a 'delayed donation', in that a donor allowed the NGO to keep and eventually sell equipment which was given for a particular project. The bank interest is a 'hidden donation', in that it is interest earned on donor funds. The genuine non-grant income is therefore less than it appears.

- The cash and bank balance are almost two-thirds of the year's operating costs. This is excessive, but donors may be to blame for disbursing cash before it is needed, and therefore allowing the NGO to avoid tight cash management.

- The purchase of the fax machine is a good example of how NGOs can use their surplus for general purpose equipment which cannot be ascribed to any one project.

- The NGO is earning a small but significant amount from the hire of its vehicles and from selling consultancy services. This shows that they are attempting to become self-sustaining, and are charging for services which most NGOs give away. These are signs of good management.

- The bank interest received is only about 4 per cent of the cash and bank balances ($2500 divided by $62 200). If the money was available for several months, it should have been placed on deposit, where it would have earned a higher rate of interest.

- The small overspending on grant-funded activities is reasonable, and is another example of a good use of surplus. It would be better, however, to make a surplus, in order to gain the advantages of partial self-sustainability which were mentioned in the last session.

6. Deal with the accounts for NGO III in the same way. Explain that the 'general fund' refers to accumulated surpluses from previous years, like reinvested profits for a business. Participants should raise the following issues, among others:

- As with the previous case, the cash and bank balances are inefficiently high, at over six months' costs. Donor money should be put to work, not left to lie in the bank.

- The NGO has a very large investment in buildings and equipment, in comparison with the level of work as indicated by the annual costs. This may not be the most effective use of the capital it has.

- Most of the expenses appear to have been incurred on administration and overheads, rather than on actual field activity.

- The NGO is making a small surplus, which means that it can survive, and it has some 'cushion' against an unexpected withdrawal of funding.

DAY EIGHT — SESSION FOUR; CASE-STUDY, NGO I

NGO I started as a branch of another NGO in 1982, and became an independent organization in 1993. It works with rural artisans to upgrade their skills and designs and it buys and resells their handicrafts and other products. The majority of the sales are to 'alternative marketing organizations' such as Oxfam Trading in the UK.

NGO I Balance sheet at 31 March 1993

Sources	$	Uses	$
Equipment donations	12 200	Cash and bank	13 900
Loan from foreign NGO	25 200	Stocks	27 000
Loan from parent NGO	37 500	Receivables	44 400
		Advances to artisans	8400
Accounts payable	21 200	Equipment	12 200
Owed to artisans	9500		
Taxes owed	300		
Total	105 900		105 900

Income and expenditure account for 12 months ending 31 March 1993

Handicraft trading		$
Sales		152 500
Opening Stock	26 000	
Purchases	134 500	
Total available	160 500	
LESS closing stocks		27 000
Cost of goods sold		133 500
Gross trading margin		19 000
Expenses		
Administrative salaries	13 000	
Bank interest and charges	1300	
Repairs and maintenance	900	
Contributions to artisan groups	3700	
Dairy Costs	4700	
Taxes	400	
Total expenses		24 000
Loss		5000
Other Income		
Transport and packing charges	5500	
Bank interest	200	
Milk sales	2300	
Subscriptions	200	
Administrative charges	1200	
Other contributions	4100	
Total other income		13 500
Net Surplus		8500

DAY EIGHT — SESSION FOUR; CASE-STUDY, NGO II

NGO II was started in 1980, and is engaged in a wide range of development programmes, including health, education, technology, income generation, energy, watershed management and environmental improvement.

NGO II Balance sheet at 31 March 1993

Sources	$	Uses	$
Capital fund	153 200	Cash and Bank	190 100
Current grants recd.	157 400	Equipment	126 100
Loan from other NGO	4800		
Staff security fund	800		
Total	316 200	Total	316 200

Income and expenditure account for 12 months ending 31 March 1993

	$	$
Grant income		253 800
Other income		
Gifts in kind	200	
Vehicle hire charges	500	
Bank interest	6500	
Sale of equipment	13 400	
Consultancy fees	1800	
Sundry donations	3400	
Total non-grant income		25 800
Total Income		279 600
Expenses		
Expenses on grant projects	253 800	
Non-grant expenses		
Overspending on grant projects	600	
Purchase of fax machine	6300	
Miscellaneous	600	
Total non-grant expenses	7500	
Total Expenses		261 300
Surplus		18 300

DAY EIGHT — SESSION FOUR; CASE-STUDY, NGO III

NGO III was started in 1974. It runs several integrated rural development projects and community health programmes, and also organizes regular training courses and meetings at the national level. It is funded from a variety of foreign sources.

NGO III Balance sheet at 31 March 1993

Sources	*$*	*Uses*	*$*
Capital fund	280 000	Cash and bank	78 300
General fund	90 400	Equipment and building	308 900
Accounts payable	19 800	Accounts receivable	3000
Total	390 200	Total	390 200

Income and expenditure account for 12 months ending 31 March 1993

	$
Income from grants	1 176 000
Bank interest income	25 000
Total Income	1 201 000

Expenses

Maintenance of building and equipment	3500
Conferences and seminars	10 400
Agricultural expenses	2500
Rural development expenses	8600
Enterprise development programmes	2700
Health centres	3100
Salaries	35 900
Rent	1500
Electricity	2600
Vehicle maintenance	10 600
Travel costs	6900
Taxes	700
Printing and stationery	3500
Transport	200
Post and telephone	2400
Newspapers and periodicals	300
Bank and audit charges	800
Education	1300
Insurance	1200
Welfare charges	400
Depreciation of equipment	37 000

Total expenses	136 100
Excess of expenses over income	16 000

Finance and strategy for NGOs

OBJECTIVE

To enable participants to identify critical operating and strategic issues in NGOs through analysis of simple accounts.

TIME

One and a half to two hours.

MATERIALS

Case study, NGO IV, or, if possible a similar case-study developed from the annual report of one of the participants' NGOs. As with the previous session, it is vital that the instructor should work carefully through the figures before the session, so that he clearly understands all the analysis, such as the ratios in item 2.

If possible the case study should be distributed the previous evening, or earlier, so that participants can read it on their own and, if possible, discuss it in their groups before this session.

SESSION GUIDE

1. If the case-study on NGO IV has not be distributed in advance, distribute it now and allow participants 15 minutes to read it on their own. Then divide them into small groups and allow them 30 minutes to identify the major management and strategic problems facing NGO IV. Stress that they must analyse the figures carefully, using the simple methods they have learned, and that they should not at this stage consider what might or should be done to remedy the problems. They should try, however, to use the results of their analysis of the figures and the written material to identify the possible fundamental 'strategic' problems which may be the real causes of the management weaknesses they have identified.

2. Reconvene the group and ask a spokeperson for each small group in turn to state the problems they have identified. Ensure there is no repetition, and list them on the board. They should include:

- The NGO has no capital of its own. All its money is borrowed.

- The stocks are equivalent to over two years' sales.

- The NGO owes its producers for one year's worth of supplies.

- There is no effective quality or stock control.

- The NGO is dependent on its founder's voluntary time and cash 'loans' but is nevertheless still making massive losses in relation to its turnover.

- The attitudes of the founder of the NGO are not appropriate for a trading operation.

ure that participants focus on the problems, and not the solutions. Management aid to be 80 per cent identifying the right problems, and only 20 per cent solving em. NGO managers, like many others, tend to spend too much time solving the wrong problems.

3. When the problems have been listed and discussed, ask participants individually to suggest ways in which the problems might be solved. Encourage a free flow of ideas, and remind participants that strategic management goes beyond keeping proper records, installing quality control systems and so on. Problems of the sort that have been identified are often the symptoms of more fundamental weaknesses, which can only be solved by radical changes. Elicit options such as the following:

- Close down the NGO, by returning such of the stock as can be returned, and paying off as many of the loans as possible. This would allow the founder to redirect his activities.

- Concentrate on a small number of handicraft products and producers, depending on the expertise of the founder, and aim to excel in these products.

- Run down the trading activity and supplement and eventually replace it with the research and other work which is now undertaken outside the NGO.

4. Stress that the NGO must make some hard decisions. An NGO trading organization which buys and then fails to resell artisans' products is not doing them a service. Eventually it will have to stop, and the producers may by then have come to rely on it rather than seeking to improve their products so that they can be marketed by a self-sustaining organization.

Discuss these options. Stress that NGOs often need radical change of this sort, and that such changes are always painful to somebody, such as the suppliers who will lose a customer or the staff and associates who are emotionally committed to a certain activity which is to be closed.

5. This is an extreme case, and the NGO on which it is based has since 1993 made radical changes. Fundamental problems of this sort can only be avoided if NGOs are always willing to question what they do and how they do it.

Ask participants if any of their own NGOs are facing similar problems, or might be but are unaware of the fact because they have not analysed the figures in the ways suggested in this session. Stress that NGOs must be businesslike if they are to be able to help people to generate income through their own businesses. They cannot hide behind their good intentions.

DAY EIGHT — SESSION FOUR; CASE-STUDY, NGO IV

NGO IV was started in 1990 in order to assist other NGOs to promote income-generating activities for their clients. It assists them with product design, development and marketing. The founder and others who are involved in the NGO also undertake research and consultancy and training projects. These activities are funded from a variety of sources, but although they are often linked to the handicrafts marketing operation, the fees received for them are used only to cover the costs of the projects themselves. The founder of NGO IV does not wish the handicraft trading operation to be cross-subsidized, and the sponsors of these projects would not be willing to allow this either. A few design, travel and training costs which are directly related to the handicraft trading are funded from government sources.

NGO IV purchases handicraft items from a number of other NGOs all over the country. They include towels, sheets, table-cloths, cushion covers, shoulder bags, bedspreads, leather bags, garments, embroidery, bamboo and pottery products, greeting cards, calendars, wood carvings, beadwork and wall hangings.

These items are mainly marketed through shops in various parts of the country, and through private contacts. The stocks are kept in a small room adjacent to the founder's residence. Previously they were kept in a room in the city which was part of a handicraft warehouse, and it was difficult to control the quantity and the quality of the goods. Some of the salespeople took goods on credit, and never paid for them. Some items proved to be substandard when they were unpacked for sale. Other items have gone missing, or been damaged during transport to and from the shops when they have not been sold. Thirty-three hundred dollars had to be written off the stock value at the end of the 1992/93 financial year because of this.

The founder does not make any charge to the NGO for the time he devotes to it, nor for the space it occupies. He believes that it would be wrong to gain from marketing handicrafts which are manufactured by needy people, and which have been supplied by other NGOs which are also trying their best to help these people. He earns a reasonable amount from his related consultancy and research projects, and he often lends some of his own earnings to NGO IV when it is in need of cash. He is not sure when, if ever, these 'loans' will be repaid.

NGO IV has never received any grants or other assistance from other sources, apart from a small loan from a charitable trust when it was started. The founder believes that handicraft marketing should be self-supporting. The founder maintains good personal relations with the staff of the supplier NGOs, and his personal 'loans' have often been used to pay the outstanding accounts, when they have asked for payment. When NGO IV started it was understood that goods which could not be sold would be returned, but the transport costs would have been excessive and it was difficult to determine whether poor quality or damage had arisen before or after delivery to the NGO. For that reason, no goods ever have been returned.

NGO IV Balance sheet at 31 March 1993

Sources	($)		Uses	($)
Founder's loan	4800	Cash		1100
Owed to suppliers	23 900	Receivables		100
Owed to trust	300	Stocks		20 600
Less loss	(6200)	Sales tax owed		1000
Total	22 800			22 800

Income and Expenditure Account for 12 months ending 31 March 1993

	$
Handicraft trading	
Sales	7300
Opening stock 6900	
Purchases 23 900	
Total available 30 800	
LESS closing stocks 20 600	
(after losses and write-offs $3300)	
Cost of goods sold	10 200
Gross loss on trading	(2900)
Non-trading income	
Design fees 4000	
Travel refunds 500	
Training fees 1100	
Bank interest 200	
Total non-trading income	5800
Net income	2900
Expenses	
Honorarium 1600	
Designers' fees 1600	
Post, phone and telegrams 500	
Travel 1700	
Transport 600	
Audit fees, taxes etc. 300	
Training expenses 400	
Exhibition expenses 400	
Welfare 300	
Printing 1400	
Miscellaneous charges 300	
Total expenses	9100
Total loss	6200

The enterprise experience: conclusion

OBJECTIVE   *To enable participants to present and share the results of their enterprise experiences.*

TIME   *One and a half hours.*

ADVANCE PREPARATION AND MATERIALS

Participants should have handed in the completed accounts for their enterprises the day before, in order to enable you to assess them and to identify the prize winner(s) with the highest profit per member and the best-kept books. If possible, you should have asked each enterprise to submit a set of accounts after three or four days' operation, to ensure that any fundamental mistakes could be corrected at that stage.

Participants should also have been asked to prepare a simple presentation for this session, summarizing their financial results, and identifying the lessons they have learned. You should have three simple prizes ready to present to the winners, ensuring that there are enough separate items to cope with winning enterprises which are owned by more than one person.

SESSION GUIDE

1. If any participants borrowed money from the course organizers, and it has not yet been repaid, they should repay it now, with any interest due, and whatever security they deposited should be returned to them. If the owners of any enterprises cannot or will not repay their loans, the security should be sold to the highest bidder from the class, and any balance remaining from the proceeds after recovering the loan should be returned to the defaulters.

This has never actually happened, but participants should understand that the enterprise experience loans, like NGO loans, are meant to be repaid. Any difficulties that arise when disposing of the security can be used to demonstrate the problems of taking effective securities from members of a close-knit community.

2. A representative of each enterprise should then present their financial results, showing the beginning and ending balance sheet for the business, and the profit-and-loss account for the complete period which explains the difference between the two sets of figures. The presentation should also include a brief statement of what the owners learned from the experience, and what changes they would make if they had to run the same business again.

3. The first prize should be awarded to the owner(s) of the business which has made the highest profit per owner. The profit should include any wages they may have paid to themselves, as well as their profit after deducting wages. If they have any equipment or unsold materials or stocks at the close of business, the value of these should be conservatively estimated for the purpose of calculating the total profit.

The second prize should be awarded to the enterprise which has the best set of accounts. These should be judged before this session, on the basis of their completeness, their accuracy and the neatness and presentation. Some of the figures may show that the participants who have prepared them still have not understood the meaning of a balance sheet. Use these examples in this or in one of the forthcoming summary sessions to remind participants of the basic principles of accounts. Remember to stress that it is you, the instructor, who has failed to help them to learn properly; those who have made mistakes should not feel embarrassed.

The third prize should be awarded on the basis of participants' voting (by secret ballot) for the enterprise which provided the best service to participants who were its customers.

4. The enterprise experience should be enjoyable, and the awards of the prizes should not be taken too seriously. Nevertheless, it is important that participants should appreciate that it is a serious learning experience, and that it should indeed have demonstrated that if lessons are enjoyable they are more likely to help students learn than if they are boring.

The experience should have helped participants to understand a number of important issues. Initiate a discussion by writing these rather extreme statements on the board, and asking whether the experience has changed their views on any or all of them.

- Formal accounting records are neither feasible not useful for small businesses.

- Individual businesses are more likely to be successful than group enterprises or partnerships.

- Business opportunities are best identified by the people who are actually going to own and manage them.

- Low prices are not the main reason why people buy things.

5. Finally, ask participants whether they can think of other groups for whom the enterprise experience might be used as a training tool. Elicit suggestions for groups such as:

- Young people who are about to leave school and who are unlikely to be able to find jobs; this can introduce them to self-employment.

- Educated unemployed young people who have been trying to find jobs for some years, and who have skills on which they might base their own businesses.

- NGO field-workers who are starting to work in enterprise development.

- Civil servants or others who are about to retire and who may need or wish to start their own businesses.

If some participants are expecting to be able to use the enterprise experience as a training tool, ensure that they are given copies of the trainers' guide before they leave.

Evaluation

OBJECTIVE
To enable participants to decide why, for whom, by whom and when their work should be evaluated, and then to select and apply appropriate measures by which to evaluate their activities.

TIME
One and a half hours.

SESSION GUIDE

1. Project evaluation for NGOs is sometimes regarded rather like record-keeping for businesses; everyone believes that it is necessary, but not many people know how difficult it is to do it properly, or how to use the results.

Ask the participants on one side of the room to pretend that they are opposed to evaluation, and to think of reasons why NGO projects should *not* be evaluated. The participants on the other side of the room should suggest reasons why NGO projects *should* be evaluated.

2. Allow participants five minutes individually to write down as many reasons as they can for the point of view they have been asked to support. Ask them for their reasons and list them on the board. Cite reasons against evaluation such as:

- Evaluation is expensive, it is often undertaken by outside consultants and it also occupies time of the NGO's own staff.

- Evaluation often distorts the results of what is being evaluated. Trainers try to amuse rather than instruct their trainees in order to get good 'ratings', credit managers make too many loans in order to achieve lending targets or extension workers make unnecessary visits in order to fulfil their quotas.

- Evaluators often interrupt clients' businesses unnecessarily when they are obtaining evaluation data.

List reasons in favour of evaluation such as:

- To find out if programmes need to be changed.

- To find out if programmes should be stopped.

- To find out if programmes should be repeated.

3. Encourage discussion, and ensure that participants appreciate why it is more necessary for NGOs to evaluate their work than it is for business people.

Business owners are forced to evaluate the quality of their services every day. If their customers stop buying, they know something has to be changed if the business is to survive. NGOs do not have the benefit of this immediate 'feedback', because their clients usually pay only a part of the costs of the services they receive, and often pay nothing at all; they will continue to 'buy' the product or service even if it is not value for money.

A tea-shop owner who gave away tea free of charge or below cost would have to ask his customers for their opinions as to the quality of his tea, since they would continue to take it even if the quality was poor. In the same way, NGO staff have to find ways of evaluating their services in addition to measuring the demand from clients.

4. Stress that it is only worth spending time and money on evaluation if somebody does something with the results. Many NGO staff believe that the main or even the only purpose of evaluation is to satisfy donors. Ask participants *who* should use evaluation findings. Encourage suggestions such as:

- They themselves, the people who are managing and conducting the programmes which are being evaluated.

- The clients, the people who are intended to benefit from the programmes which are being evaluated.

- The donors, the people who have paid for the programme.

Many evaluations are in fact produced only for donors. Stress that they should be the last and probably the least important users of evaluations.

5. Having decided why and for whom programmes should be evaluated, participants should now say *when* they should be evaluated. Elicit a range of suggestions such as:

- Continuously, while the programme is actually being conducted.

- When a service for a given client is completed, such as a trainee when her training is finished or a borrower when he has finished repaying a loan.

- At the end of a project.

- Some time after the end of a project, such as harvest time or a year after a training course.

Evaluation is often regarded as a one-time exercise, to be undertaken on one specific occasion only. Stress that it is a continuous process. Ask the participants how you yourself are evaluating this very session, as you are speaking now. You are watching the participants as you speak to them and are unconsciously evaluating your own performance. You are using the 'feedback' messages you are receiving from their expressions to prevent them sleeping, or being bored or confused.

The long-term results of many programmes cannot be measured until many months or even years have passed. The benefits from investments such as schools, roads, irrigation works or even a course such as this one are only realized in the very long term. It is clearly impractical to delay evaluation until all the benefits are revealed, but this shows that total evaluation is impossible, all one can do is to obtain whatever indications are available at each point in time, and make appropriate improvements accordingly.

6. Now ask participants *who* should evaluate development projects. Are the external consultants who are often called in by donors the only people who are qualified to evaluate NGO activities?

Participants should appreciate that projects can and should be evaluated by everyone who plays any part in them. The most important and reliable evaluators, who can most rapidly and effectively act on the results of their own evaluation, are:

- The clients who are intended to benefit from the projects.

- The NGO staff who undertake the projects.

Headquarters managers and external consultants have a role to play, but clients should be encouraged to monitor continuously the quality of the service they are receiving. Field-workers should use client reactions, and other monitoring tools, continuously to assess the quality of their own activities, and should automatically correct and improve their work on the basis of this feedback.

7. Participants have now identified the reasons *why*, *for whom*, *when* and *by whom* their projects should be evaluated. Only now should they consider *how* they should be evaluated. The actual measures which are used will of course depend on the type of programme. Ask each participant individually to write down one indicator by which she would choose to evaluate this training programme.

Ask each in turn to read out what they have written, and write them on the board, putting them into an approximate order of immediacy, as shown below. If necessary, encourage further suggestions in order to provide a full range such as is shown. Do not at this stage explain why you are putting them in this sequence:

a. Number of candidates applying for the course.
b. Number of participants actually attending the course.
c. Participants' informal reactions during the sessions.
d. Participant A,B,C,D session ratings given at the end of each day.
e. Tests or examinations during or at the end of the course.
f. Participants' final evaluations on the last day of the course.
g. Participants' statements of how they will use what they have learned.
h. Participants' feedback at various dates after the course.
i. Participants' employers' feedback.
j. Number and quality of innovations introduced by participants.
k. Reactions from participants' clients.
l. Actual benefits to participants' clients.

8. Ask participants to try to explain the sequence. Help them to see that the earlier indicators can quickly and fairly easily be obtained, while it takes months or years before the later ones become evident, and it can also be very difficult even to obtain the information after a long period. What then is the point of trying to evaluate a course by the later indicators. Why should training institutions not be content with one or two of the earlier indicators, as indeed many are?

Initiate discussion by asking participants to recall the objective of this course. Was it 'to hold a course' or 'to achieve a certain level of participant ratings'? Clearly it was not. The objective is to enable participants to be better at helping their clients to start and sustain viable enterprises, and to do this at a reasonable cost. A full classroom, or good session ratings, are no guarantee that this objective is being achieved. Ask participants to examine the list on the board more carefully. Which indicators actually measure results in terms of better participant performance?

Encourage the answer that many of the earlier indicators only measure 'inputs', such as course attendance or immediate participant reactions. Courses of this kind do not usually include tests or examinations, but these too are only very indirect indicators of the eventual results. Students who obtain good marks are by no means always the most successful people in their careers.

Help participants to appreciate the dilemma which arises because the 'best' indicators of results are the most difficult and the slowest to apply. There are no 'right' and 'wrong' evaluation indicators, and project managers have inevitably to make a compromise between the quickest and easiest but least meaningful indicators and the slowest and most difficult but most valuable ones.

9. Ask participants to suggest similar 'hierarchies' of indicators for other types of projects in which they are engaged, such as savings and credit schemes, sanitation or health programmes or general community development. They should relate these to the programmes they are themselves running, and will select measures which appear to balance the need for reality and the need for feasibility.

Preparing and presenting proposals

OBJECTIVE
To enable participants to prepare and to present to potential donors convincing proposals for programmes they wish to undertake.

TIME
Two and a half to three hours.

SESSION GUIDE

1. Ask participants whether preparing and presenting proposals is part of their jobs; some field staff may say that it has nothing to do with them. Stress that in a participative organization every staff member should contribute information and ideas for the preparation of important proposals, and that they will only be able to play a useful part if they have some understanding of what is involved. They should also be able to make proposals for changes within their own organizations. Even a simple new idea has to be effectively communicated if it is to be accepted. The same principles apply to any sort of proposal, presented at any level, inside or outside the organization.

Ask participants to suggest why so many NGOs fail to obtain funding for their projects, even when they have good ideas and their clients desperately need their assistance. Participants may suggest that lack of money, political interference or lack of contacts are the problem.

Stress that donor organizations have enormous sums of money which are budgeted for the types of projects which NGOs are capable of undertaking, and many of them fail to spend the money that has been allocated. Very often, the main problem is lack of communication between the NGOs and the donors. What is the main channel through which an NGO can communicate its ideas to prospective donors?

Participants may refer to 'networking', which is indeed important, but effective personal contacts are not enough. Project proposals are the chief formal means of communication between NGOs and donors. Many NGOs which work in enterprise development are unable to prepare and present effective proposals, and this is perhaps the main reason why so many good potential projects are never funded, and why so much donor money is unspent.

2. Ask participants, particularly less senior staff in larger NGOs, whether their own or their colleagues' good ideas are always adopted, or even properly presented, within their organizations. Many NGOs, even very large ones, do not use formal written proposals as part of the process of assessing ideas which are put forward internally by staff, and formal presentations are in any case only a small part of the total decision process. Nevertheless, the effort of thinking through a new idea and writing it down in a coherent way can very significantly improve it. The process which participants are about to experience is a valuable part of project design as well as an important part of 'selling' new ideas, within or outside organizations.

Divide participants into small groups. Tell them to imagine that they wish to run a

169

course such as this one, and they have to prepare a written proposal to solicit funding from donors, or, if this is more appropriate for their positions in their respective NGOs, to solicit the necessary funds from their seniors within their own organization.

Participants must decide on the main topic headings they will include, and on the approximate number of pages, or fractions of pages, they will devote to each topic. Stress that they should not concern themselves with the content of the proposal, but should merely decide on the structure and approximate length.

3. Summarize the assignment on the board, and allow up to 30 minutes for its completion. Reconvene the groups, and ask each in turn to present their answers on OHP or flip-chart sheets. Summarize the heading titles in columns on the board, to facilitate comparison. The actual words used, or the sequence, are not important, but each group should include the following topics in its list. They may have combined some with others, but the basic content must be covered.

The following list is based on one particular set of guidelines. This is of course by no means the only correct list or sequence, and opinions will differ as to the appropriate length depending on the nature of the project and the extent to which the donor is already familiar with the NGO making the application.

a. Summary
A brief statement of the name of the NGO, the location, the nature of the project and the clients, and the amount of money that is being requested (half a page).

b. The organization
A description of the NGO which is making the proposal, including its official registration, its history, the names of other donors and some evidence to demonstrate its competence to undertake the type of project that is being proposed (one page).

c. The clients
An account of the clients whom the project intends to assist, where they are located, their current condition and their problems (half a page).

d. The project
A brief description of the nature of the project, its objectives, any other organizations which are involved, the planned activities, the expected results and how the activities, or the results if appropriate, will be sustained after the end of the project (one and a half pages).

e. Evaluation
How the project will be monitored and evaluated, and how the donor(s) who fund it will be kept informed of its progress (half a page).

f. Timetable
A schedule of the project, starting from approval of funding and running until completion and evaluation (half a page).

g. Management
A description of how the project will be organized, managed and staffed, who will be directly responsible for it and how they are qualified for this task (one page).

h. Finance
A budget of the resources needed, including contributions in kind or in cash from the clients and from the NGO, and showing how much money is being requested from the donor, and when it will be needed (one page).

i. Assumptions
A statement of the assumptions on which the success of the project will depend, and of the risks which must be taken into account (half a page).

4. Some groups may have included other topics, and most will probably have allowed considerably more than the total of seven pages given in the above outline. Ask them to justify any other items, and ask why a proposal that is too long may often be worse than one which is too short. Ask participants to imagine themselves to be staff members of a typical donor organization who receive large numbers of proposals every week. What will their needs be, as 'customers' of the NGOs? How will they react to unnecessary material?

Donor staff want to be able to form a judgement as quickly and easily as possible. If the necessary information which they need to make a decision is buried within pages of repetitive material, or is not available at all, the proposal will probably be rejected without further consideration. Most donors do not have the time or the staff to investigate any but a small proportion of the proposals they receive, particularly from NGOs with which they have not had previous contact.

5. Go through each of the headings in the list, and ensure that all participants understand each one. Some in particular may be unfamiliar to most of the participants, and the following points should be stressed.

a. The summary is perhaps the most important part of the proposal, and is nevertheless often altogether omitted. It is the first thing that the donor reads, and it enables him to decide which department the proposal should be sent to, since many donors have different staff to deal with proposals from different areas, covering different types of activity or for different sums of money.

b. The organization; the 'track record' of the NGO is almost certainly the main factor which determines whether project proposals are approved or not. The proposal should say something about the leaders of the NGO, and a copy of the up-to-date audited accounts should be appended to the proposal if the donor has not previously funded its proposals.

c. The clients; many projects do not actually assist the poorest people whom most donors wish to help; such people may be helped only indirectly, through obtaining employment for instance, but the proposal must clearly state who it is hoped will benefit. Many proposals contain pages of general description of the wretched condition of the proposed 'beneficiaries', without any clear information as to how many of them will benefit, by how much.

d. The project; many lengthy proposals fail actually to state what the NGO is actually going to *do*. Donors need to know what they are being asked to pay for, and exactly what the results are expected to be.

e. Evaluation; remind participants of the earlier section on evaluation. This section of a proposal should reassure the donor that the NGO will itself continuously monitor the progress of the project. The donor will also be regularly informed as to progress, without being burdened with too much unnecessary information.

f. Timetable; many proposals fail to give any indication of when the project will start or end, or they may give a starting date which is only a few days after or even some time before the prospective donor receives the proposal. This tells the donor either that the NGO management is being quite unrealistic, and has no idea of the time it takes for donors to make decisions, or to organize and start a project; or that the proposal has been unsuccessfully circulated to many other donors before.

g. Management; more projects fail because they are badly managed than for any other reason. Donors need to know how the NGO will cope with the extra administrative load that any new project necessarily involves, and how the project itself will be managed. They may have confidence in the leader of the NGO, but even the best leaders can take on too much.

h. Finance; donors are aware that projects are more likely to succeed if their clients, and the NGO, make some contribution to them, possibly in terms of labour hours or other facilities other than in cash, rather than relying entirely on donor funds. Donors also need to know when the funds will be required, for their own cash-flow management, and are also aware that managing new projects usually involves increased overhead costs. If a proposed budget omits any allowance for increased management, this suggests that the managers are not aware of the need for it.

Separate budget headings should also be included for major items, but it is important not to give a false impression of accuracy, or to break down the expenditure into unnecessarily detailed items. Everybody knows that it is impossible to estimate the exact amount that will be spent on postage or stationery, and if a proposal includes apparently precise estimates of such small amounts, as well as large sums to be spent on vague and unexplained items such as 'administration' or 'travel', prospective donors will be suspicious.

i. Assumptions; no project can be guaranteed to succeed, and a good proposal should indicate the risks that are involved. A course such as this one, for instance, however well it is run, may fail altogether because participants' organizations will not allow them to make any use of what they have learned. If a proposal shows that the NGO's management are aware of the risks, this suggests that they will do their best to avoid them.

6. Ask participants to suggest how the above headings and space allocation might be changed for proposals for different types of project such as health, irrigation or credit. Stress that the basic topic headings need not be changed. The proposal may be rather longer, but supplementary material such as maps, detailed descriptions of project areas, construction estimates or evaluation reports on past achievements should not be included in the body of the proposal. They can be enclosed as

appendixes, so that donor staff can take them for granted, read them, or pass them to appropriate experts, as they think fit.

7. Ask participants with experience of obtaining donor funding how they select the donor to whom a specific proposal should be sent, and how, if at all, they adapt proposals to specific donors. Encourage the following guidelines:

- The best prospects are those donors with which the NGO is already in contact, and from which it has previously received funds.

- Different donors have different priorities. Some are more concerned with different areas, or different issues, such as health, gender, the environment or enterprise development.

- Some donors work on different financial years than others, some prefer to co-fund with other donors, and some have different preferences for the layout of proposals. NGOs must market themselves effectively by catering to different 'customer' requirements.

8. If possible, show participants some examples of badly typed letters or badly printed publicity material from an NGO, and ask them to compare this with neatly but inexpensively prepared material.

Stress that good presentation does not necessarily involve computer word processing or expensive plastic binders. Even a neatly presented handwritten proposal can be far more effective than a sloppy but expensively prepared document with many typing errors, pages bound upside down and so on. This only demonstrates waste and incompetence, and suggests that donor funds will be similarly wastefully used.

9. The course has been designed to remind participants over and over again of their responsibility to make use of what they are learning, in order to yield a satisfactory return, in terms of benefits for their clients, from the investment they, their employers and their sponsors have made in the training.

Participants should have been warned well before this session that on the last day they will have to prepare and present a proposal for a new project or for modifications and improvements to an existing programme. If a number of people come from the same organization they may prepare and present their proposals in small groups not exceeding four participants, but they should otherwise make individual presentations on behalf of their own organizations.

Remind participants that they will have the opportunity to apply what they have learned in this session in their presentations the following day. The details of the assignment are as follows:

- Prepare the outline of a proposal for a project which you believe should be implemented by your NGO. This may be a new project, requiring donor funding, or it may be an internal change or improvement, requiring only the re-allocation of existing resources.

- Be ready to make a 15-minute presentation of your proposal, to your colleagues on the course and to a panel of representatives of senior management from NGOs, sponsors and donors or other authorities.

- The actual document need not be prepared, but the outline of the proposal and the main facts should be included. If basic data such as costs or client numbers are not available, you should clearly indicate what information you need and how you will obtain it.

10. Participants should use whatever time they have available after this session, and the first session of the following day, to prepare their presentations. When making them they should be encouraged to make effective use of flip-chart sheets and other presentation materials. They should be encouraged to share and discuss their ideas with one another, whether they are from the same NGO or not, and the instructor should be available to counsel and advise them as needed.

What next?

OBJECTIVE

To enable participants to practise their proposal presentation skills and to benefit from informed comment on whatever projects they plan to introduce on their return to work.

TIME

Three hours or less, depending on the number of presentations.

ADVANCE PREPARATION

A small panel of three or four 'judges' should be asked to attend the presentations, and to comment on them. These can include senior management from NGOs, sponsors and donors or other prestigious and well-informed authorities. Participants should have been given sufficient time, and facilities, to prepare convincing presentations, following the guide-lines given in the previous session.

This session is the culmination of the course, since it provides an opportunity for participants to draw together what they have learned and to expose their ideas to a critical panel of outsiders. The session should therefore be in some way 'set apart' from the rest of the course. It may be possible, for instance, to have it in a different location, and some other observers apart from the panel of experts may also be invited.

Nevertheless, it is important not to lose the sense of commitment to future action in a mass of ceremonial. This, like all the sessions, should be businesslike, and any official closing ceremonies should be kept to a minimum, in order to avoid giving the impression that the end of the course is the end of the effort that has to be put into it. The real work starts when it is applied.

The panel members and any other visitors should be given lists of the participants, and participants should also have been told who the panel members are. They may also be asked to request a particular panel member should be asked to comment on their presentations.

SESSION GUIDE

1. Introduce the participants, panel members and any visitors to one another, and briefly explain the purpose and general content of the course.

2. Depending on the number of presentations to be made, each individual or group should be given 15 minutes to present their proposal, and a further ten minutes for questions and feedback from other participants and from the panel members.

In order to ensure that participants maintain their interest in their colleagues' presentations rather than worrying about their own, it may be useful to warn them at the beginning that after each presentation you will nominate one participant to comment on a particular aspect of it. The questions might be selected from the following:

- Was the sequence and content of the presentation clear?

- If you were a prospective donor, would you be certain as to how much money you were being asked for, and when it would be needed?

- Did the presentation suggest that the NGO is aware of the need for management of the timing of cash inflows and outflows?

- Were you told who the expected beneficiaries would be?

- Is the total cost of the project reasonable in relation to the benefits which are expected to result from it?

3. After participants have asked questions and made comments, ask one of the panel members who has a particular interest in the area or the NGO in question to comment. Here too it may be useful to ask specific questions, such as:

- Does the project appear to be feasible; can it be done?

- Which donors might be expected to look favourably at the proposal?

- Which particular aspects of the project should be emphasized, for which donors?

- What additional information is needed?

- Are the evaluation and reporting arrangements appropriate?

- If you were a donor, would you recommend acceptance of the proposal?

Invite the other panel members to ask further specific questions or make comments as they wish.

4. When all the participants have made their presentations, ask the panel members to comment in general on what they have heard. The presentations should have given them some idea about the emphasis and content of the course, and they should be asked frankly to criticize the approach to enterprise development and to project presentation that has been adopted.

Finally, thank the panel for their time and their views.

Course evaluation and follow-up

OBJECTIVE

To enable participants to apply to this course what they have learned about evaluation, both as a practical lesson and in order to assist the instructor to improve the course in future.

TIME

One to one and a half hours.

ADVANCE PREPARATION

Participants should have been asked after each two- or three-day period, and certainly at the end of the first week and after session two on this the final day, anonymously, to rank each session on the following scale:

A = Excellent   B = Good
C = Mediocre   D = Waste of time

The collated results of these simple immediate evaluations should be available for this session, together with blank copies of the final evaluation form following the layout given at the end of this session guide.

SESSION GUIDE

1. Remind participants of the earlier session on evaluation. Why is it appropriate to devote one of the final sessions of this course to evaluation even though there are as yet no real results at all, since only the costs have been incurred so far? The benefits will only come later, when participants' apply what they have learned.

Encourage the response that you, the instructor, need to learn from the participants how you can improve the course next time. You will also be obtaining further more meaningful evaluation data, later, but the various sessions are now fresh in participants' memories and you wish to find out as much as you can from them.

Ask how most school or university courses are evaluated. Who evaluates whom? Teachers evaluate students, by tests and examinations. These may or may not be an effective way of finding out if students have learned to *use*, as opposed to write about, the things they are intended to have learned, but a trainer in enterprise development, like any NGO worker, must evaluate himself.

If our clients do not benefit from our assistance, we must change it. If trainees do not learn what we have tried to teach them, we must improve their teaching and the design of our courses.

2. Distribute the final evaluation form and ask participants to complete it without any discussion, to ensure that their views are not influenced by an articulate or talkative minority.

While they are completing this, or before if possible, collate the most recent individual session ABCD ratings. Then go through all the ratings for the whole 10 days of the course, and identify those sessions which were rated significantly worse than the majority, and certainly any which received fewer A and B ratings than C and Ds.

3. Collect the final evaluation forms. Put them to one side and list on the board the less-popular sessions you have just identified. Go briefly through the list, and ask participants whether the sessions were badly rated because the topics were irrelevant, or because they were badly taught.

It is most unlikely that any sessions will be badly rated by every single participant. Ask those who were in the minority and rated the unpopular sessions A or B to identify themselves, and to defend the sessions in question. They may be unwilling to do this, but it is important to recognize that opinions can differ, and that a few positive views can suggest changes of emphasis which will improve the majority rating next time.

Be prepared for and indeed invite criticism of your own performance, NGO staff have to learn to learn from their clients, and to improve their performance on the basis of such feedback, and you can personally demonstrate this behaviour in this session. Ask participants what changes they would recommend, and ensure that these are noted and taken seriously. State clearly that badly rated sessions will be substantially changed or omitted and make it clear that their evaluation is more than a cosmetic exercise.

4. Ask participants to write down in one sentence the most important thing they learned during the course. Allow five or ten minutes for this, and while participants are doing it, leaf quickly through their final evaluation forms in order to identify any common themes or particularly striking comments.

5. Ask participants to put their notes of the most important thing they learned to one side, and to recall what they wrote in the final evaluation form a few minutes earlier. Go through the responses one by one. Invite those who presented a minority view, whether it was positive or negative, to identify themselves and to explain their opinions, and ask for further comments as appropriate.

Participants in courses of this kind usually ask for more additional topics to be included than for unnecessary ones to be omitted, but they may also suggest that the course should be shorter, or at least no longer, and that the daily workload should be reduced. Point out the inconsistency of this view, and invite suggestions as to how the course might be restructured without increasing its duration, and thus its cost and inconvenience to participants' employers.

Summarise the changes you believe you will make, after a first hearing of participants' views, and thank them for their comments.

6. Ask participants one by one to read out the main thing they learned during the course. Summarize their statements on the board. If the emphasis is different from what you intended, ask why, and remind participants that they are your customers. What they have learned is what they needed to learn, and they should ensure that the course is a good investment by applying it on their return. The following session will give them an opportunity to state how they propose to do this.

DAY TEN — SESSION FOUR

Final evaluation form

(Note: Do NOT write your name on this form)

What was the best part of the course? ....

....

What was the worst part of the course? ....

....

The course was too long/too short/ right length (delete as appropriate)

What topic(s) might have been omitted from course? ....

....

....

What topics might have been added to the course? ....

....

....

What comments have you on the administration before and during the course?

....

....

What comments have you on the accommodation and eating arrangements?

....

....

Any other comments (continue overleaf if necessary)? ....

....

....

Summary and conclusion

OBJECTIVE *To enable participants to draw together what they have learned, and to commit themselves to a specific action, which they will undertake on their return home, and thus to maximize the chances that participants apply some part of what they have learned in the course when they return to work.*

TIME *One to one and a half hours.*

ADVANCE PREPARATION

The proposals which participants presented on the previous day will probably involve decisions by other staff and perhaps donors if they are to be successfully implemented. Participants should also have been regularly reminded that improvement and change only come about if individuals, of whatever level, make a conscious effort to improve what they themselves do, without anybody else being involved.

Distribute two copies of the action commitment form to each participant one or two days before this session, and ask them to bring the completed forms to this session, and to be ready to make a two- to three-minute presentation of what they propose to do. Stress that they may, and probably should, commit themselves to something quite modest or even trivial, such as bringing certain records up to date, visiting one more client or even cleaning up an office so that it is a more efficient work place and a more welcoming environment for visiting clients.

The commitment may or may not be a part of the project which participants presented during the 'What next?' sessions. It must, however, be something which participants believe they can achieve on their own, without important new resources having to be made available from others in their organizations.

SESSION GUIDE

1. Remind participants of the initial exercise when they were made aware of the cost of the course, and the necessity to earn a commensurate return. This final session is the end of the spending and the costs, and should be the start of the earning and the benefits. The course at this point is like a machine which has been paid for and installed but has never produced anything, or a bicycle which has been bought but never used to go anywhere. What would they say to a client who bought a sewing machine with a loan but never used it?

Ask participants to describe what they usually do on the first day after they return to work from a course, or from any long period of absence. They have to pick up the threads, to answer letters, to write reports and to fit back into the domestic and office routine. It is very easy to allow this 're-entry' process to obliterate all memories of the course, however relevant it may have been.

2. This session aims to provide a 'bridge' between the course and the job, and to increase the chances that participants will start to apply something of what they learned, even on the first morning at work.

Experience has shown that if somebody makes a small change as soon as possible, it will be easier for her to make more important changes later. It is very easy to say what we cannot do, because we need other people's agreement or assistance, but it is more difficult, and far more productive, to say what we can do, on our own. Large-scale improvement only comes from individual small-scale efforts, and participants should remember the famous saying: 'Nobody ever made a greater error than he who did nothing because he thought he could do so little.'

3. Remind the other participants that what they learn from and with one another is more important than what they learn from the instructor. Warn them that after each presentation you will nominate one participant to comment on his colleague's action commitment, so that everybody will have the opportunity both to present and comment on somebody else's effort.

Stress that their comments should be positive. Enterprise is about optimism and seeing opportunities where others see problems. It is easy but unhelpful to say why things cannot be done, and comments should be like:

'Yes, that is a good idea, and have you thought about how you could extend it (or do it more quickly, more economically, etc.) by doing . . . ?' or

'That would be wonderful, but you will need Mr X to co-operate. Why don't you try approaching him through Mrs Y; he usually listens to ideas from her.'

4. Ask each participant in turn to come to the front of the room and briefly to summarize his action commitment, stressing in particular the verifiable point he will have reached by the date specified on the form. Allow two to three minutes for this, and a further one or two minutes for comment and questions, initially by the nominated respondent, and then by other participants who may wish to assist.

5. Be sure to collect the spare copies of the action commitment forms. Remind participants to keep their own so that they will not forget what they have committed themselves to.

Ask for suggestions as to what you can do to help participants fulfil their undertakings. Encourage suggestions such as:

- Write to their employers, summarizing the commitment and recommending support for it.

- Write a reminder to each participant a few weeks before the expiry of the period.

- Hold a one-day reunion seminar a few days after the expiry of the period, to put participants under pressure to fulfil their commitments, and also to provide general follow-up support.

You should have ascertained before the session what you can do to follow up the action commitments, and also to evaluate the post-course performance and to plan for future training. There is always a danger that the only result of a course is

181

another 'follow-up' course. A short seminar may be useful, but stress that improvement in the field depends ultimately on participants themselves.

There is also a tendency for field staff to use their seniors' reluctance to accept new ideas as an excuse. Stress that change in organizations comes from 'below' as much as from the top, and they must have the courage and determination to promote the improvements they believe in.

Tell participants what you are going to do to support them, and reinforce the sense of commitment by reminding them yet again of their responsibility to their clients.